Marie Pea

THE WAY OF LIFE

A GUIDE TO THE ETHERIC WORLD

giving 419 extracts from the verbatim records of sittings with John Campbell Sloan, the famous Glasgow Direct Voice Medium, taken from the works of, and arranged

by

ARTHUR FINDLAY

First Impression 1953
Second Impression 1954
Third Impression 1955
Fourth Impression 1956
Fifth Impression 1958
Sixth Impression 1960
Seventh Impression 1962
This Impression 1986

ISBN 0 947823 06 9

Two of the foremost publishers in the psychic sphere have combined their talents to produce this most important series. They are:

THE HEADQUARTERS PUBLISHING COMPANY LIMITED. Booksellers, publishers of books and two Spiritualist monthly magazines "TWO WORLDS" and "HERE AND THERE."
5 Alexandria Road, West Ealing, London, W13 0NP.

PSYCHIC PRESS LIMITED. Booksellers, publishers of books and the weekly "PSYCHIC NEWS."
20 Earlham Street, London, WC2H 9LW.

Printed in Great Britain by
WBC Print Ltd, Bristol

CONTENTS

ARTHUR FINDLAY wrote some of the finest books on Spiritualism. Other books in the series are:

On the Edge of the Etheric
The Unfolding Universe
The Torch of Knowledge
Where Two Worlds Meet
The Rock of Truth
Looking Back
The Psychic Stream
The Curse of Ignorance

FOREWORD

WHEN an inhabitant of the world to which we pass at death was once asked, by a lady present at one of Mr. Sloan's séances, what his work was, he replied that he was attending a University. When asked what he was learning he replied: "I am learning the Way of Life." Surely no better answer could have been given, because knowledge of the way of life comprises everything to do with life, and to each of us life is our all.

After bringing together all the extracts given in this book, it occurred to me that *The Way of Life* would be a suitable title for it, as it embraces life and its meaning, both here and hereafter. The Way of Life: how much these four words mean, not only as to how we live, but as to what life is, its meaning, its course, and its purpose. The way our life is lived on earth, and in the hereafter, is a matter of supreme importance to us, and from whom could we get better advice than from our friends who have lived on earth and passed on to a larger, fuller, life in the world beyond? With their wider and greater experience, who better could be our teachers and our guides? What they have to tell us will be found in the pages which follow.

A guide to life, here in the flesh and hereafter in the etheric body, has always occupied the attention of mankind since writing and books were invented. To have something in writing, to which one could turn for help and guidance in this troubled world, has been a source of comfort and help to untold multitudes, but only within the last century has it been possible to obtain accurate information and the opinions of those who have gone before. Now we have a reliable guide to the way of life here and hereafter, and are not dependent on ancient writings by ancient scribes, who put down the thoughts and speculations of priests and theologians who made up by their imagination what they lacked in knowledge.

Those who live in what are called Christian lands are well aware that for many hundreds of years Christendom has relied on *The Holy Bible* as its guide to the world beyond, about which it tells us very little. The word Bible is derived from the name of the town of Byblus, on the coast of Syria, as there the first book was produced in an alphabet which was invented by the Egyptians. So the Greeks called this novel production a biblion and, when speaking or writing of more than one, they used the word biblia. Consequently we now have in the English language words such as bibliography, or the history of books, and bibliolater, a worshipper of books, the French using the word bibliothèque for library.

What we now call *The Holy Bible* was one of the first books to be printed on paper after the invention of printing in 1446. In those days there were few authors, and for long it was the only book read by most people in Protestant countries. Hitherto it had been written in Latin, but now it was translated into the languages of Europe. Consequently, what we call the Bible, or the Book, took a place in literature far beyond its merits. As it had no competitor in Europe of a religious nature, claims were made for it which were quite baseless, but, as no one knew better, they were accepted, and still prevail in our own times.

The Christian Bible came into being in the 6th century, when the Hebrew scriptures and certain Christian documents were brought together as one book. These writings comprised many different traditional and religious articles which were written by various authors. Jerome completed his translation into Latin of the Hebrew and Greek documents at the end of the 4th century, but it was not until the 9th century that we find the Bible in the shape and form approximating our present day Bible, though many textual changes took place when the Authorised Version was produced in 1611.

From this time onwards it was regarded with ever increasing reverence, so much so, that from the time of the Reformation it has been looked upon by Christians as holy and inspired by God, every word true, the acceptance of its saviour being considered as our only way of salvation. On the other hand the Jews remained wedded to the Hebrew Scriptures which to them is their Word of God.

Other nations have had, or still have, their sacred books, to which they have given different names. The ancient Egyptians had their Bible which in English we call *The Book of the Dead*, believed by them to have been written by their god Thoth, the scribe of the gods. This is a collection of religious texts, but its origin is shrouded in the mists of remote antiquity. It taught that those who passed, in their etheric duplicate bodies, successfully through the Judgement Hall of the god Osiris, the saviour and judge of mankind, entered a life of everlasting celestial happiness. The characteristics of this life were so similar to those of this earth that death was regarded by the Egyptians as the entrance to a new life which was just a continuation of this one, but in more beautiful surroundings.

In India, that garden of religions, we find *The Bhagavadgita*, meaning the song of the holy one, wherein Krishna, the Hindu Christ, expounds the doctrine of his faith in lofty and highly poetical language. Herein he is made to claim adoration as the incarnation of the supreme spirit. Moreover, the Hindus have the oldest Aryan scripture which they call *Veda*, meaning knowledge. The Buddhists likewise have their sacred book, *The Lalita Vistara*, a legendary life of Buddha, besides a collection of poems occupying a space twice as great as the Christian Bible, including a small collection of hymns and the ritual for the admission to the faith.

Further east, in China, the practical Confucius produced a moral and social system. This way of life found its way into a book written by his grandson, to be known as *The Doctrine of the Mean*, another being *The Great Learning*, written by the most profound of all his disciples, and this claims to contain many of the great teacher's precepts.

Up to within the last few hundred years all the phenomena of nature were believed to be under the control of divine beings, whom Homer, in his *Iliad* and *Odyssey*, the oldest surviving specimens of European speech, made so real to the ancient Greeks that these epic poems were as beloved by them as are nursery stories by children. These poems, based on the accumulated traditions of past glories and valorous deeds, rich with the joy and the dignity of man, were the sacred writings of the Greeks who believed that every word was true and inspired from heaven.

The sacred book of the Moslem faith, the youngest of the world's great religions, is *The Koran*, meaning in Arabic "recitation" as Mahomet claimed that it was a repetition of what he had heard from God. *The Koran* is the foundation of Islam, and few other books have had such an influence in moulding the opinion of great multitudes living in many lands, in fact it is rightly claimed to be the most widely read book in existence. It is not quite so large as the New Testament. Throughout most of the book God is claimed as the writer, just as we find in the Old Testament, whose prophets, like Mahomet, disappear as human personalities, to be represented as the divinely inspired instruments of the deity.

The ancient Persians likewise had their sacred book, *The Avesta*. This revealed to them the way of life and salvation, and others, of other lands, could be mentioned, but the foregoing can be looked upon as the leading sacred books of the world. They have helped and comforted multitudes, though some of these books have been used by the intolerant to crush out individual thought and create an era of cruelty, savagery, and totalitarianism over large parts of the world.

However misused some were, all, with the exception of the writings about Confucius, which were purely secular, originated in the fact that man is an etheric being. The mystics, the theologians and the mediums of the past, put into writing their thoughts on the meaning of this great truth, and, however much they misrepresented this profound subject, they were all reaching out in their attempt to fathom, to the best of their ability, the mystery of God and of human existence.

The coming of Spiritualism has changed the numerous gods of the ancients into men and women who once lived on earth, and I give them the name of Etherians, their dwelling place being called Etheria. In the past they communicated with man on earth, to produce the religions and bibles we now know, but their communications were mutilated by our ancestors, who mentally were little better than children. Few knew how to read or write, and those who could do so took no permanent careful record of what was said. Accuracy in recording remarks and events was very uncertain, and, when these doubtful records reached the hands of the theologians and the mystics of those days, the people of the other world were imagined as gods who ruled the earth and all creation. Imagination was not curbed by rational thought.

Consequently, the priests put into the mouths of these divine beings the speculations and theories of their own simple minds, and, what has come down to us is not the communications of the men and women of Etheria, but the theories which priestly minds attributed to God and the gods. So these old sacred books are of little help to us, and represent only the beliefs of an ignorant mystical priesthood, who, because they knew no better, burlesqued a simple truth which Spiritualists now hold in all its purity.

Since 1848 careful records have been made of some of the supernormal happenings in the presence of mediums. These include the utterances of mediums in trance and what is called automatic writing, when the hand of the medium writes with no effort, and what is written is not the medium's own thoughts. These reports were possible because trance and automatic writing mediums speak and write in the light. On the other hand, direct voice mediums, such as Mr. Sloan, held their séances in the dark, to enable what is called "ectoplasm", which they give off, to materialise the Etherians' vocal organs. As light hinders this, all the séances recorded in this book took place in darkness.

The darkness required for a good long sustained direct voice séance, means that few verbatim records have been taken of what has been said at these séances in the past. The sitters have had to depend on their memories, but here in this book this difficulty has been overcome by the two stenographers who reported in the dark all that was said at the séances herein recorded. This being so, we now have the exact words spoken by the voices of the Etherians who communicated, and we are no longer dependent on what comes through trance and automatic writing mediums.

We cannot imagine a better way of speech than by an Etherian's own voice. By the voice we communicate with each other on earth, and, if we could only see the Etherian when he is speaking, there would be no difference. Sometimes these other world people are seen when speaking, but full bodily materialisation uses up so much ectoplasm that they save it to enable them to carry on their conversations. In the case of the séances here recorded, which lasted from two to three hours, some Etherians took from five to ten minutes to say what they had to tell us.

Considering how few direct voice records have been made in the past a book such as this is unique. Instead of having to read what was said, or written, through the mouth, or hand, of a medium, we now have the exact words recorded which were spoken by the Etherian communicators themselves. Nothing has been added and nothing omitted.

Instead of going back to ancient times to read what ignorant and childlike priests had to say on the way of life, and such vital matters as life and death, we can now read for ourselves what our friends who have passed on have to tell us. They have made what has always been regarded as the dreaded journey, and now they come back and tell us what it is like, what they are now like, and what kind of place they now inhabit.

This book is not for the purpose of recording evidence to settle the identity of those who spoke. That was carefully and satisfactorily done, and the evidence will be found in some of my other books. Likewise, personal names on this and the other side have been omitted as far as possible. This book's object is educational, and for the purpose of informing us of the way to live on earth, and on the things which will come our way after death. The information was given by those on the other side whom I, and the other sitters, learned to trust, and I have every reason to believe that what they said was accurate.

The bibles of the past claim to have been inspired by God, or the gods, but this claim lacks evidence and is obviously untrue. Age does not make for truth, and dust cannot gather thick enough on books to make them reliable. What we know at the present time is much more valuable to us than all the speculations of the past. Consequently, the new outlook on life on earth, on death, and on our life hereafter, as given in this book, should be a help to many, and I hope it will be accepted as a revelation of the way of life, the way it should be lived, and its eternal meaning.

ARTHUR FINDLAY.

Stansted Hall,
Essex.

VISIBLE AND INVISIBLE VIBRATIONS

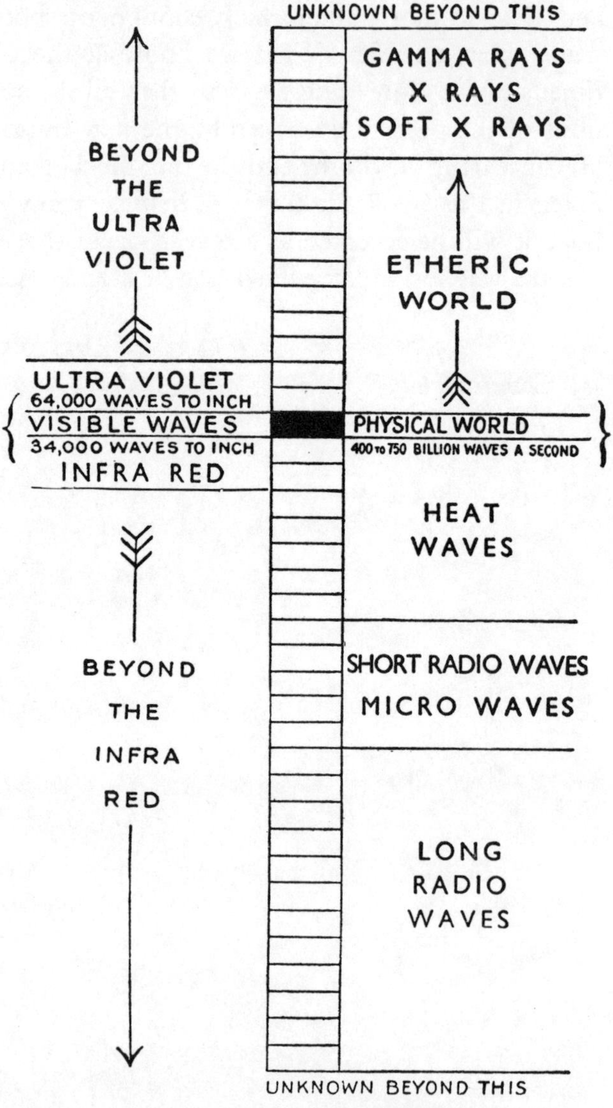

The above chart makes clear how limited are our sense perceptions. Only the black portion represents the visible spectrum. This is all we sense of the innumerable etheric waves making up the Universe. The author has been told by his informants in the Etheric World that its vibrations just about touch those of the Physical World, and at times they can be detected by clairvoyance, by the seeing of etheric beings, called ghosts, and by psychic photography. Etheric waves, however, seem to be different from physical waves as so far we have discovered no instrument to contact them.

PART ONE

CHAPTER I

INTRODUCTION

HISTORY records down the ages many so-called movements for the reform or advancement of political or religious beliefs. A number of people, with an outlook different from that generally prevailing, got together, and they were considered by their contemporaries to be peculiar or unorthodox.

In such a way political and religious reform movements have started, to develop, or fade out, or be suppressed by the government. Some, like Christianity, or the Labour movement, became large organisations, and then they were accepted by the people as respectable, and were no longer abused.

The Spiritualist movement is like so many others of the past. First it was denounced and then accepted, first it was considered as contrary to the will of God, and then made legal by Act of Parliament in 1951, when the Fraudulent Mediums Bill gave Spiritualists the religious liberty denied them since the 4th Christian century.

The reason for this reform was because, over thousands of years, the evidence in favour of supernormal phenomena had increased, to become so impressive that more and more people came to realise that there was evidence of not only a visible universe, but also of an invisible universe, one in which there was life, intelligence, and movement.

The Spiritualist movement had many pioneers, and the records of some of their abnormal experiences have come down to us in history. In fact, the oldest story of a materialisation and the direct voice occurs in the epic of Gilgamish, the King of Sumer, where Abraham was born, which is some 4,000 years old, the story being written on baked clay, which has not been tampered with over all these years.

Records of abnormal happenings occur in ancient Egyptian literature, and we have Plato's record of the sayings and doings of Socrates, which makes clear that he was a medium. In Greek and Roman times séances were held, and Livy, Cicero, and Tertullian record super-normal happenings, which they attributed to the spirits of the dead.

Both the Old and New Testaments, *The Koran*, and ancient religious literature contain psychic stories, and it is evident from the records which have been preserved that Jesus, Mahomet, Apollonius of Tyana and Apuleius, besides many others who lived in the early part of the Christian era, had psychic power, and would have been looked upon to-day as mediums.

During the first four hundred years of the Christian era, mediums were called the "Oracles of God", to become thereafter insulted by the name of "Servants of the Devil", because of the decree of Pope Damasus, who was influenced by his secretary, now known as Saint Jerome. The belief in witchcraft was thus encouraged, to bring about the persecution and death of many thousands who undoubtedly had psychic gifts, but the ignorance of these times was such that they were looked on in fear, as those who had sold themselves to the devil.

In European history two outstanding trials of mediums are recorded. So we know from the questions asked, and the answers given, exactly with what these two women were charged, and what they had to say in their defence. The first trial, that of Joan of Arc, was in 1431, and the second, that of Bessie Dunlop, of Lyne, Ayrshire, in 1576, reveal that these two victims of the Christian Church were mediums of the first order, the first being clairaudient and clairvoyant, the other a direct voice and materialisation medium. Both these were burnt to death at the stake.

The first outstanding medium of the Christian era to escape persecution or death was Emanuel Swedenborg (1688-1772), a leading mining engineer, and this may have been caused by his high social position, his father being a nobleman and a Bishop of the Swedish Church. He was undoubtedly the "John the Baptist" of Spiritualism, which was brought to the prominent notice of the public in the following century by the extraordinary phenomena experienced at Hydesville, in the State of New York.

Continual rappings in their house disturbed both Mr. and Mrs. Fox and their daughters, and, as so many others who visited them likewise heard these noises, which spelled out words and sentences, one rap for A, two for B, and so on, one committee after another was set up to investigate the cause. From that time onwards, mediumship became accepted and respected in the United States of America, a medium coming to Britain in 1852 to make some notable converts.

These rappings first occurred in 1848, and, because of the impetus they gave to the study of supernormal phenomena, the year 1848 is looked upon as the year of the birth of modern Spiritualism. From that time onwards the movement has grown enormously, and it must be a source of satisfaction to the early pioneers, now in the other world, to contemplate the progress of their beliefs in a little over a hundred years.

Let us think for a moment of the position of thought one hundred years ago. Then, the Christian Church in Europe, North and South America and the Colonies, was the dominant influence outside of politics. It purveyed what it called the only revelation received from heaven, and, by teaching that all unbelievers were eternally damned, it had an iron grip on the mind of Christendom.

All sections of the Christian Church taught similar doctrines, and its opinion about life after death was gloomy in the extreme, even for believers. Then the Church taught, as it still does, that we are in the grave, asleep, until the Resurrection day at some uncertain future date, when, in our physical bodies "at the last trump", we will all be gathered before God's Throne to be judged, the believers in Church doctrines being ushered into a fantastic heaven, and the unbelievers being doomed to the torments of hell for all eternity.

If some Christians think otherwise to-day it is because of the influence of Spiritualism on modern thought.

About the same time that the Spiritualist movement was born, Charles Darwin published his famous book, *The Origin of Species*, in the year 1859, which was the beginning of the undermining of many of the claims made by the Christian Church.

So much was this so that an age of materialism began, to become the recognised mode of thought amongst the majority of scientists and intellectual thinkers. To them, as explained by Ernst Haeckel, the famous German biologist, man is a monism quite lacking the power to survive death. In other words, according to this teaching, which took hold of so many thinking people, man is not an immortal being, but only a creature of flesh and blood whose consciousness is confined to the period between birth and the grave, after which all consciousness is extinguished.

The Rationalist movement, which gave such support to this outlook, had certainly the effect of exposing the fallacy of the numerous superstitions and supernatural claims made by the Church throughout the Christian era. For that, all men and women who have the welfare of humanity in mind should be thankful, but alongside the Rationalist movement worked the Spiritualist movement, which has put before mankind an outlook different from any other.

Spiritualists realise that the Church has misunderstood and misused events which originated in psychic phenomena, for the purpose of producing and supporting its many false dogmas and doctrines. This began in an age of the darkest ignorance, and has prevailed during centuries of little knowledge and education. Then, no one knew any better, but now most thinking people realise the error which has been taught, and how the Church, by its exclusion of mediumship from the church services from the 4th century onwards, was unable to teach the people aright with regard to their life hereafter.

From the time Jerome and Pope Damasus, in the 4th century, excluded mediums from the early Christian Church, the ignorant multitude had nothing more to rely upon than the dictates of a Holy Church or a Holy Book, which latter, amongst Protestants, took the place of the Pope, the Holy Father.

The Spiritualists, on the other hand, by getting back to Natural religion, gave a new interpretation to all religions by discovering that the origin of every religion was the same, namely, psychic phenomena, around which theologians all over the world had spun their creeds, dogmas, ceremonials, and ritual.

Because psychic phenomena is sporadic and cannot be made to occur at will, the phenomena which brought every religion into being was gradually superseded by error and superstition, controlled by a powerful force of ecclesiastics whose interests were to keep the people ignorant and fearful.

Consequently, there grew up this autocratic priesthood which made itself responsible for the religion of the people. They decreed what was to be believed, and in general those who thought for themselves were persecuted, banished, imprisoned or put to death.

That was the position in Western Europe up to the beginning of last century, but the great advance science made during that century brought about such a reaction amongst thinking people, that orthodox religious beliefs were cast aside as superstition and the priests lost their highly exclusive position and power.

The scientists, relying only on what they discovered, and dealing only with physical matter, became materialistic in their outlook, some going the length of denying the reality of what some call the soul and the existence of an invisible etheric world.

Consequently, during the 19th century Materialism and Spiritualism grew up together, the one denying the soul in man and an etheric universe, while the other affirmed them.

Both Materialists and Spiritualists, however, agreed in acknowledging the error in supernatural orthodox religion, but no amount of proof that psychic phenomena is a reality could induce orthodox science to consent to its examination. A few scientists did examine the claims made by Spiritualists and were satisfied, but, taken as a whole, the scientists were adamant that the belief in psychic phenomena could be classed on the same plane as the superstitions of religion.

All the same, Spiritualists have more than held their own, and nothing the scientists have said or discovered has disproved the claims of Spiritualism, in fact, the science of physics has made understandable the claims made by Spiritualism. So we find ourselves to-day somewhat in the following position:

The Christian form of belief appeals to an ever-lessening number of adherents, but Christians refuse to believe the claims made by Spiritualists, who, by many orthodox Christians, are still considered to have strayed from the right path and gone contrary to the will of God. The Materialists, on the other hand, consist of those who have never seriously examined the subject, and, in their ignorance, condemn it as due to fraud and folly.

Nevertheless, the Spiritualists are receiving more respect as each year passes. Some fifty years ago it was impossible to talk in public about psychic matters, whereas to-day they are very often the topic of conversation. As the number of mediums grows, more people will become interested, and obtain further knowledge of the subject. Then, by reading the works of those who have investigated, the knowledge will gradually become more diffused until ultimately the Spiritualist outlook on life will be accepted.

We cannot expect the belief in Spiritualism to come from the investigations of the scientists, who, contrary to all scientific principles, refuse to investigate something which they have already determined to be impossible. That attitude is quite contrary to true scientific methods of research, which combine investigation and research, observation and experience, towards all aspects of natural phenomena. To take up the position, without investigation, that certain phenomena cannot take place is so unscientific as to be sure of ultimate collapse as ignorance decreases.

Spiritualism, while discarding all the superstitions which have gathered around supernatural religion, the legends and mythology, the ceremonial and the ritual, is steering the middle course, keeping to that which is true, and that which can be proved by experiment. Meanwhile, the orthodox in religion accept by faith and not by proof, while the scientists reject both faith and proof.

This half-way course is the one which the Spiritualists believe will ultimately leaven the ranks of the supernaturalists and the materialists, so much so that some day we may look forward to religion being accepted as based on the proofs and discoveries made through mediumship. Established facts must ultimately prevail. Thus will Science and Religion some day come together.

It is impossible to mention the names of the pioneers of the Spiritualist movement, both men and women, in this country and in America. Men and women from all walks of life have helped to enlighten mankind. Some have held high positions, and had considerable influence throughout the land, while others did what they could in their own neighbourhood to spread what they considered is the truth.

Spiritualist churches and psychical research societies have been springing up over the past hundred years throughout the English-speaking world. In the large towns throughout Western Europe, and in most of the larger and smaller towns of the United States and Britain, one or more Spiritualist centres are to be found, either for worship or for research. In Brazil, the extensive movement there has been directed by the writings of the Frenchman, Allan Kardec. He, however, influenced the thoughts of his followers more to the doctrine of reincarnation than to the belief in progress advanced by both American and British Spiritualists, and he gave mediumship little consideration.

Spiritualism stands for the fact that life does not die at death and that the so-called dead, who are still men, women and children like ourselves, are actively alive in another world surrounding and interpenetrating this one. Spiritualists know this, because their friends who have died have returned to them, and at times been seen, but more often heard, when certain natural conditions have been observed to make this possible.

Not only can they speak to us through the use they make of the medium, but they can also hear what we say to them, and thus make conversation possible. From these conversations Spiritualists know (1) that, to begin with, their friends are still much the same in form and character as they were on earth, (2) that everyone reaps what he sows, but progress is open to all, and (3) that our friends who have died are often with us and can know much of what takes place on earth.

Spiritualism is consequently a natural, and in no way a supernatural, religion, because it is based on personally experienced facts. Moreover, these give satisfaction and comfort, besides contributing an urge for increased mental and ethical development. We are mind, and mind never dies; death is a door, or a bend in the road of life, and not a wall or a dead end.

The creed of the Christian faith contains no ethical or moral instruction, and is no guide to the way of life. Spiritualism, on the other hand, is a guide to the way of life, as we know from those who have gone before that here and now we are preparing the place we shall occupy in the other world. As we live here our mind is making for each of us the conditions in which we shall live hereafter, as it is character, the quality of the individual, that counts, and not belief in creeds and dogmas.

Spiritualism is natural religion, based on facts and evidence, and it is to be hoped that in time, when its teaching is better understood, it will help to raise everywhere the moral and mental standard of mankind. Those who call themselves Spiritualists believe that it can be accepted as true that:

(1) The universe is governed by Mind, commonly called God. That all we have sensed, do sense, or will sense, is but Mind expressing itself in some form or another.

(2) The existence and identity of the individual continues after the change called death.

(3) Communication, under suitable conditions, takes place between us here on earth and the inhabitants of the etheric world, into which we shall all pass at death.

On these three fundamental principles, which Spiritualists believe can be reasonably accepted, the following logical deductions are naturally drawn from the information which comes to us from those who have passed on to this larger life.

(4) That our ethical conduct should be guided by the golden rule, given first to the world by the great Confucius, "Whatsoever you would that others would do to you, do it also unto them".

(5) That each individual is his own saviour, and that he cannot look to someone else to bear his sins and suffer for his mistakes.

(6) That each individual reaps as he sows, and that he makes his happiness or unhappiness just as he harmonises with his surroundings. That he gravitates naturally to the place in

the etheric world in harmony with his mental development and desires, as there aspirations can be gratified more easily than here on earth.

(7) And finally, that the path of progress is never closed, and that there is no known end to the advancement of the individual.

What follows in this book amply bears out these Seven Principles of Spiritualism, so that they need not be further elaborated here, but before closing this introductory chapter, let me say something about vibrations, a subject to which those who speak to us from the other side so often refer. The science of physics embraces the knowledge of the make up of matter, or the constitution of substance, in other words, it tries to answer the questions some would like to know, namely, what makes up the physical universe, the suns, stars, planets and this world on which we live.

During this century our knowledge of this subject has increased enormously, and we now find that it makes possible the correct understanding of the problems which face us when examining the youngest of all the sciences which is known as Psychics, the science dealing with the invisible universe which is around and about us. To understand Psychics we must first know something of Physics and, as the word vibrations is so much used by Etherians in the pages which follow, let me briefly state the latest opinions of science on the constitution of physical matter. This will help us to understand better about the etheric substance of which the invisible etheric world is composed.

We live and move and have our being in a physical world which is composed of substances vibrating within certain fixed limits, to which we give the name "matter". We are born into it, and we accept it as if it comprised everything, and yet how different things are from what they seem to be. Matter which looks so solid is in reality not solid at all. What we see when we look at a table or a chair, for instance, are the vibrations of a certain number of electrons, which are revolving at immense speed around a centre known as the nucleus. Matter is made up of atoms, and these atoms are in turn principally composed of electrons and protons. According to the number of electrons in an atom so is the substance, but the weight is conditioned by the number of protons.

In iron, for instance, there are always twenty-six planetary electrons, and consequently, when we look at or handle something composed of the foregoing, we sense something to which we have given the name of iron, or, to put it correctly, when our eye is affected by the ether vibrations these electrons create, we form the mental image of iron. Our touch is likewise affected by the vibrations these electrons produce, and they give us the effect of heat and cold, but the number of protons gives us the sense of weight.

Physical matter is in reality an open network of electrons and protons, and the distance between the electrons and the protons in an individual atom, in relation to its size, is immense. If we consider the nucleus as commanding the same position in an atom as the sun does in our solar system, then the relative distance the electrons are apart from one another, and from the protons, might be taken as equivalent to the distance the planets are from each other and from the sun.

Again, if we consider an atom as somcthing the size of a village church, then a pin-head would represent the size of one of the electrons of which it is composed. These protons and electrons in the atoms are thus far asunder, moving at enormous speed, and they are linked together by the invisible ether which occupies much the greater space within the atom.

Matter is thus constructed of minute electric charges, both positive and negative, not moving haphazardly, but freely and orderly, and connected together by the invisible ether which some believe to be the basic substance of the universe. We imagine the ether filling all space, though, as we cannot grasp space, we are unable to comprehend its extent. We know, however, that the ether waves can undulate through space at the rate of 186,000 miles a second, which undulations, or waves, give us what we term light. Under certain circumstances the vibrating energy of these waves of ether can be translated into equivalent energies of heat and electricity.

Though we cannot see the ether yet we infer that such a substance exists, because heat, light and electricity travel through space at a definite rate, and therefore there must be a medium through which they undulate. Our physicists therefore argue that the ether is a pragmatic hypothesis, a logical postulate.

This invisible substance is the medium between things material and our senses, but matter is now considered to be this same ether in certain fixed states of vibration. The electrons in the atoms are particles of negative electricity, and the protons are certainly electric in their nature. Both are etheric, and matter is only ether in a particular condition. All ether is potentially matter and all matter potentially ether. Physical matter, which appeals to our senses, is only that section of the ether which happens to be vibrating within certain fixed limits.

The ether of space can now be taken as the one great unifying link between the world of matter and that which we term etheric, as it is the substance common to both worlds. Both are contained within this substance, both are part of it, and both are formed out of it. The two worlds are part of the same universe, and life in both is conditioned by it.

Here, in this world of matter in which we function, we are conscious of a lower scale of vibrations, whereas in the etheric world, where life also functions, consciousness is affected by a higher scale of vibrations. The ether is as much to other life in the universe as it is to us. To this other life its surroundings are just as substantial and real as ours are to us. Life functions in the ether, and it is just as much able to do so when free of matter as it is when clothed in matter; in fact, a fuller, larger life can be imagined when the physical body is discarded.

As we proceed, these views will be better appreciated, as in the communications from those in this further life, which I shall report, it will be seen that they tell us that the etheric world is just as real, just as tangible, just as beautiful, in fact more so, than the world of physical matter which appeals to our limited sense perceptions.

Only the ignorant affirm that just what we sense is

real, that beyond this range of sense nothing exists. Our range of sense, our sight, our touch, our smell and hearing are limited to the last degree. We know that the spectrum of the spectroscope proves the very limited range of our ordinary vision, and that further ranges of vibrations of what would be colour, could we see them, extend on either side.

It has been said that the perceived vibrations, as compared with the unperceived, are much less than is an inch to a mile. Therefore it is evident that there lies an enormous region for other life to inhabit around and within this world of ours, a region quite beyond our normal sense perceptions. (See Chart at end of book.)

Until we clearly understand that our senses here only respond to a very limited range of vibrations, namely those we term physical matter, that outside these there is a universe full of life, which responds to a higher range of vibrations, unreal to us, but more real to it than physical matter, we cannot grasp or understand in all its fullness the psychical phenomena which develop through mediumship.

About and around us, interpenetrating this physical world, there is another world into which we pass at death. It has been described to me by those who have spoken to me from it, but only in language suited to our minds accustomed to respond to the vibrations of physical matter.

When asked how best to explain it to others I was told to compare it to a sea of ether, wherein personal movement is even more rapid and easy than that of a fish in water. Let us take, for example, the sea in which are floating sponges entirely submerged. Surrounding these sponges is a medium which supports life, and so the etheric world can be contrasted with water surrounding our earth, except for the difference that the sponge absorbs only some of the water, whereas the etheric world is not only outside our earth but inside as well. Interpenetrates is the only word we have to describe something real inside something else which is real, and it is on a surface of this etheric world we shall some day live.

We are so made that in the physical body we are in harmony with physical surroundings. At death we leave our physical body and function in our etheric body. We pass into the new environment which surrounds us, an environment which supports life, just as water supports life. We on earth are in this sea of ether, though we know it not, and just as much now as we shall ever be. The difference death makes to us is not so much a change of location as a change of appreciation. We now only appreciate the physical, but then we shall appreciate the etheric.

Only when we desire to do so shall we again get into touch with the physical, as the physical pertains to physical matter, and the etheric to etheric matter, each in its own order, the one difference being that they of the etheric world can come back to us at will, see us, and appreciate us and our surroundings.

We can but listen to what they tell us and try to imagine. We are somewhat like a blind person here on earth. We seldom see these men and women of the etheric world, but conditions can be produced which enable us to hear them, and from what we are told imagine as best we can.

Sitting in the séance-room listening to the Direct

Voice can be likened to sitting at home listening to the Radio. We hear the speaker but we cannot see him. Nevertheless we accept the voices from the Radio, and they influence our minds and imagination, just as do the voices which speak to us at a Direct Voice séance.

Moreover, we hear someone speaking on the other side of a wall, and our mind reacts to what he says and he can hear us reply. So we can have a conversation, which means that the unseen person is there and can think in the same rational way as we do. Because we do not see him we do not think that he is not there, in fact, we are quite certain that he is there.

So our mind likewise reacts to what is said at a séance by personalities who are unseen, but are nevertheless very real, and, like the person on the other side of the wall, they think rationally as we do. They hear us, can converse with us, argue with us, laugh with us, and so on. In fact, they are just human beings like ourselves, invisible to us, but nevertheless very much all there. Moreover, what they have to tell us is of vital interest to everyone.

With this introduction to our subject, let us now proceed, and I hope everyone will appreciate how easy and natural were the conversations from which the extracts, or quotations, here given have been taken, just as did those who were present at these memorable séances.

CHAPTER II

THE MEDIUM

I HAVE written and spoken much about Mr. John Campbell Sloan in some of my books and on public platforms, but then I was able to write and speak of him as one of us on earth. Unfortunately for us, but fortunately for him, he passed on in May 1951 at the age of eighty-two. Since his passing he has come back several times to say how happy he is in his new home, and that he has met many of the Etherian men, women, and children, who came to his séances to talk to us on earth.

A short biography of this famous medium will be found in my book *Where Two Worlds Meet*, and in *On the Edge of the Etheric* I tell of how I came to the conclusion, after sitting with him on thirty-nine occasions, that the phenomena which took place in his presence were supernormal. In both these books I explained how he was the passive reservoir, drawn on by the people on the other side who required a substance from his body which enabled them to materialise their vocal organs and speak to us on earth.

When I had my first séance with him in 1918 I knew nothing of Spiritualism, and naturally thought that the different voices I heard speaking were either his own or the voice or voices of one or more accomplices. That was natural, because I had never heard of ectoplasm, which is the name given to the substance they draw from his and the sitters' bodies. I knew nothing of our etheric body, which is a duplicate of our physical body. This body I learned passes out of our physical body at death, along with our mind and memory, so that we are the same person after death as we were before it, except for the loss of our material body.

This, and much more, I gradually learned at his séances, so much so that I discovered a new invisible, but very real, world about us to which we passed at death. Then I was told that the people who live there once lived on earth, and could materialise with this ectoplasm their duplicate etheric vocal organs and speak to us on earth. So I now had a natural basis to enable me to understand how speech was possible, and how voices could be produced without our physical vocal organs, but that did not satisfy my enquiring mind. I must be certain before I could believe this, and that it was not the medium or someone else on earth who was telling me.

So I decided to have sittings alone with Sloan, and I took with me my own stenographer to record everything said. I made sure that the voices did not come from her, as she sat in another part of the room where she could hear everything but, if she spoke, I would know. Elsewhere in this book I tell of how I satisfied myself that when the voices spoke it was not the medium who was speaking, but besides that there was the evidence given by those who spoke. My relations and friends came back and spoke to me, recalling events that only they and I knew. Much was said that it was impossible for Sloan to have found out, even if he had had the time to do so, which he had not.

He went out to work early in the morning and he worked on his allotment plot in the evening. He read little because of his poor eyesight, and his intelligence and general knowledge were that of an average artisan. Gradually I realised all this, and besides that I found he was a man of high character, a man to be trusted and respected. His only fault was his grumbling and grousing, but this was more amusing than irritating. Tact and patience were required, and they generally succeeded. He was quite indifferent to money, and no one was ever asked to pay for being present at one of his séances. He gave these because he had a high sense of duty, and his pleasure came from the comfort and satisfaction his visitors obtained from the evidence they received that their friends, once looked on as dead, still lived and came back and spoke to them.

For over forty years Sloan exercised his mediumistic gifts without payment, and more will be said of them as we proceed. Even when an old man, at the age of seventy-six, his mediumship maintained its brilliance, when his memory was so poor that sometimes he found it difficult to look after himself. At times he had to be accompanied by someone when he went out for a walk or to the various houses where the séances were held, and once, when he went out alone, he was lost and could not remember the way home.

In his younger days the séances were mostly, but not always, held in a room of his own house, but after his wife's death he was invited to the houses of the regular sitters, and still the same phenomena took place. He brought nothing with him, and on arrival he would walk into the room where the séance was to be held and sit down and talk to the people present. Then the light was put out. So no preparations were made beforehand, except that in Summer the window was previously darkened by the hostess to keep out the daylight.

Until well on in middle age he always went into trance during a Direct Voice séance, but in his later life he was normal throughout the entire sitting, hearing the voices and carrying on conversations with those who spoke to him. After his wife's death in 1940 he received much comfort and satisfaction from the talks he had with her, and this was possible because the operators of the séance on the other side found that they could produce the voices equally well when he was normal as when he was in trance.

So the following remarks, which were made about him, were spoken when he could hear and reply to what was said, but they only refer to what was said about his mediumship, and omit the conversations he had with his wife, and other friends on the other side, which will be found in their right place.

The mass of correct evidence which was contained in the conversations between the sitters and the Etherians is not given in this book, which is confined only to what was said of an educational nature. The evidence of identity of the speakers can be obtained in some of my other books, but this one is for the purpose of recording those things which we all ought to know. Once the identity of the speaker was established, as it was in most cases, what he or she said concerning the other world, and their way of life, is of value and well worth preserving. Mediums of

Sloan's brilliance are rare, and it is unfortunate that much more that was said at his séances has not been recorded. There was enough to have filled very many books the size of this one.

What follows in this chapter concerns only the remarks some Etherians made about Sloan's mediumship, and the first to be given came about when there was a conversation between an Etherian and a gentleman sitter. This is what the Etherian had to say about the medium:

"Any time I come to you in these surroundings I am dependent on the human element—the friend whom you call John Sloan. Without him, or one equally gifted, we could not make you hear us, but although you do not hear us unless he is present, we do come back and watch over you from time to time. He is just the vehicle for the transmission of sound. I could not speak to you if I could not draw from you collectively."

One night the sitters were discussing mediumship amongst themselves, during a lull in the conversation with our friends on the other side, when the strong manly voice of an Etherian gave his name, and spoke to his wife who was present as one of the sitters. This is what he said, and it was only too true:

"Yes, John Sloan opened the door, my dear old friend Sloan, to Eleanor and me. We were treading a lonely way, Eleanor—you know the time when we were up against a stone wall, so to speak, and the dear old friends (Mr. and Mrs. Sloan) came down and we heard Bobbie speak. I will never forget that night. God bless you."

Bobbie is their son, and his father returned at a later sitting.

"God bless you, Daddy Sloan. My God, you opened the way of life to me completely. If it had not been for you, I would never have known this truth. I will never forget the night when Bobbie first spoke to us."

Then he turned to his wife and said:

"Do you remember, Eleanor?"

"Yes, dear, I remember," replied his wife, "but you have him beside you now," to which remark her husband replied:

"Yes. I am beside him now, but it was my dear old friend here who changed my outlook on life, and made God real to me."

The mother in Etheria of a lady present, who knew Sloan when she lived on earth, was always grateful for the opportunity she got at these séances to speak to her daughter. Once, after giving her name, she spoke to the medium and said:

"God bless you, John Sloan. It is to you that I owe so much."

"I have done nothing for you, but you were a dear old soul," replied Sloan, to which she answered:

"And many will say you were a dear old soul also. I wonder sometimes, if you can catch the intonations of my voice?"

Another lady in Etheria, who gave her name, the mother of one of the sitters, who had sat with Sloan in her earth life, once had a talk with him. "My, I am glad to hear you speak," Sloan said, to which she replied:

"I think you are a wonderful man, John Sloan.

You brought some beautiful thoughts and aspirations to us when we did not understand properly, but it did us some good when we came to this side of life."

An old friend of the medium, a man who had passed on, once returned. He gave his name, and the two had an amusing talk about old times. Then the Etherian, speaking to everyone, remarked:

"It is a constant source of wonder to me to understand why I can speak to you here so that you can hear me. I think I must be speaking very clearly to-night, because I sometimes come into your surroundings, not only here but in your home, and talk to you in the same manner as I am speaking at present, but you do not appear to hear me. I must give the credit for you being able to hear me now to our old friend here. (John Sloan.)"

Sloan always belittled his mediumship; he was one of the humblest of men, and never took any credit to himself for the marvels which happened at his séances. On one occasion something he said brought this remark from an Etherian:

"He is the instrument through whom we are able to prove that we do not cease to exist although we are out of the physical."

At another séance, when Sloan said that his power was going, and that he was now too old to be of any use, a voice from the other side called out:

"You have reached a degree of perfection, my friend, that you have never realised you possessed."

At one séance, the husband in Etheria of a lady present first gave his name and then had a long talk with his wife. He spoke for several minutes and concluded with these words:

"That friend of yours, and of mine, John Sloan, through whose gift I am enabled to speak to you, I send him my grateful thanks. My voice may sound different to you, but I know, when I see your face lit up with that recognising smile, you know who I am. Good night, my dear."

The fiancé in Etheria of one of the sitters once addressed the medium in these words:

"There have been many letters which you have written, my friend Sloan, and many letters have been written to you, tributes which will live long beyond your passing from the earth side of life. Yes, I know, Mr. John C. Sloan, and now that I am over here I know what a difference it would have been to me had I just been a little less sceptical in earth life. You see, I did not believe in anything of that kind at all. John Hardman speaking. I had to alter all my views when I came here. It is a hopeless life to live on earth with no hope, no prospect of any life beyond. Still, I struggled through, but what I missed in that struggle. Yes, I have got into the light which never fades."

Sloan's son was a frequent speaker. Once his father spoke to him about his unexpected death, and said how little he thought that when he said good-bye to him at the Docks it was for the last time. His son replied:

"It is just as well we do not know these things, Dad, but just wait until the time comes when you come over beside us. We will go over all the glorious scenes of the past, and walk in the new country and the new land which God has prepared for all His children. I am Dougal Sloan. If you walk according to God's laws you will have a wonderful life in the land of light. God bless you. Thank you, Dad, for you were a good Dad to me. I know you miss Mother, but she is here, and it will be all right. We will all meet again by and by. Just you go on and do the best you can. You have got strength in you yet for a while."

Once when speaking to the medium during a lull in the conversation with our friends on the other side, a gentleman present remarked that all the comfort and satisfaction that Sloan had brought to thousands would be a joy to him in the years to come. An Etherian agreed that this would be so, in these words:

"It will be a beautiful memory he will have when he comes to the other side, to know that he has brought hope and joy into the hearts of many."

As I have already said, Sloan always disparaged his mediumship. At one of his last sittings, during a silence, when he was seventy-six years of age, his rheumatism bad, his eyesight poor, and his memory failing, but when his mediumship was as good as it had ever been, he made his customary remark which everyone knew so well, "I am nae use at all." At once an Etherian rebuked him in these words:

"You take a sombre view of things. We know all about you, friend Sloan. I do not think you have a right to say that. You should allow your friends to say whether you are any good or not. I am quite sure you are very, very helpful in many ways yet. You have the power to bring comfort to those whom you come amongst."

With the above remark I shall close this chapter, which I trust gives the reader an idea of the man whose ectoplasm enabled our Etherian friends to vibrate our atmosphere, and tell us of the wonders in store for us all. Many men, who have been the leaders of the people for their good or ill, have been accounted great by their contemporaries and by historians. Sloan, from a worldly point of view, was not a great man and, had I not recorded elsewhere some of the happenings at his séances, he would have been known only to the comparative few who had been enlightened by attending them.

Nevertheless, though his death was ignored by the national press of this country, and only those who knew him mourned his passing, he was a really great man. He helped thousands to find comfort and satisfaction, by the knowledge they obtained through his mediumship that their friends still live and are happily awaiting the reunion some day. Likewise they learned that, if we live aright, we shall share the joys and happiness our departed friends are experiencing, in a world where beauty and happiness exist unrealised by anyone still on earth.

Like all great men, he had a gift which raised him above the rest of the human race. Because he was unlearned, simple, and lived a retiring life, his work for humanity was ignored, but some day, when the curse of ignorance passes, and the great value of mediumship to the people is recognised, John Sloan will be hailed as one who did more to comfort and satisfy their inmost longings than most of the so-called great of the past or present.

His work goes on through the records which have been preserved of some of his séances. These will be a satisfaction to very many in the years to come.

CHAPTER III

THE STENOGRAPHERS

SÉANCES have been held since early times. As already mentioned, we have the story of the séance held by Gilgamish, King of Sumer, some four thousand years ago. Séances were held in ancient Egypt, in ancient Greece, and by the Hebrews and Romans. A general description has come down to us of what occurred, but nothing reliable of what was said by the people of the other world. We have the story of the materialisation of Samuel in the presence of King Saul, the story of the séance held on the day of Pentecost, and the record of Tertullian in 211 A.D. about the séances held in his church, but that is all. We have nothing reliable about what Samuel said to Saul, or what the entranced disciples said at Pentecost, or what Tertullian's medium said when entranced during the services in his early apostolic church.

We are told that the early church father Jerome was annoyed by criticism made at a séance, by Etherians, about his translation into Latin of the scriptures, but never do the exact words said by them come down to us, and the reason is obvious. Few knew then how to record speech in brief handwriting quickly enough in those days, in fact, the art of shorthand, or stenography, was generally unknown until the 19th century. The Greeks and Romans had systems known to a few, but these did not survive. Not until the Reformation was the art revived, probably for the purpose of recording sermons, but the different systems in use were clumsy, inefficient and laborious.

It was in the year 1837 that Isaac Pitman produced a system which was simple enough to be easily written and read. Since this invention of modern shorthand the entire position has changed, so much so that speech can now be easily reported as quickly as the words are spoken. Consequently, of late years stenographers have been employed to an ever greater degree to record what was said by mediums in trance, or when giving clairaudient messages, but the darkness necessary for the direct voice has prevented many records being made, as taking down shorthand in the dark requires some practice.

So far as this book is concerned, I am indebted to two ladies, Miss Millar and Miss Dearie, both accurate and expert in the art of stenography, for overcoming the difficulty caused by the darkness, and for all that is herein reported as being said by those who spoke from the other side. That their records are strictly accurate there is not a doubt, because they were carefully checked within a day or two of each séance by those who were present at the séances recorded. The regular sitters always received a copy of the records after each sitting, and no one ever found anything inaccurate or questionable. In every case they were passed as correct. What is reported as being said was said, and the high characters of these two ladies, who took down the shorthand notes, is a further guarantee of their accuracy.

Some of the speakers on the other side expressed

their admiration from time to time of the way the stenographers did their self-imposed task, their work, moreover, being given without charge.

This is what one Etherian once said:

"You are a wonderful little lady, Miss Dearie. Your service to others in recording our words will be amply rewarded."

Another Etherian once said:

"It is a high honour that we can claim you as our helper, to portray our thoughts";

and on another occasion this was said:

"Whatever words you write will live after you, my dear."

A longer and encouraging statement was once made to Miss Dearie:

"I appreciate your thoughts and your work, and your sacrifice for others in writing all these things down. You don't just know what a blessing they will bring to somebody needing enlightenment and sympathy. There is never a message you receive from the spirit side of life that is not important. If it comes from the spirit side of life it comes for a purpose, and for an object in view, and it never returns home again without having fulfilled that mission."

I shall give just one more remark, made by someone from across the borderline:

"Oh, I wish I could just bring all the loving thoughts that those about you now seem to have for you. May the strength of the Great Ones give you power in your hand for a long time, my dear, to portray those beautiful thoughts from the other side of life which we have not the power to portray if it were not through the instrumentality of your beautiful thoughts and writing."

It is evident that the work done by Miss Dearie and Miss Millar was appreciated by those Etherians who spoke to us at the séances reported in this book. The thanks of all who attended these meetings go out to them both, and I have little doubt that the many thousands who read their records will feel for them equal gratitude, for the great work they did for humanity in preserving for all time everything that was said at these remarkable séances.

CHAPTER IV

THE ETHERIC BODY

THE first lesson in Spiritualism is that we have an etheric body, a duplicate of our physical body. The etheric body interpenetrates the physical body during earth life, and leaves the physical body at death. Our mind does not die, and it controls the etheric body through the etheric brain. What is called our subconscious mind shaped our body on earth, and will shape and direct our etheric body in Etheria. It constructed our earth body out of gross matter, and it has even greater power over the finer matter of the other world. The individual mind is the greatest factor in the universe. Without mind the universe would cease to be. Life and consciousness would end, and without these there would be nothing.

To be able to live after death without a body, such as we now have, is difficult to imagine and, on the first favourable opportunity, I asked what kind of a body each of us has after death. To my question the answer was given in a loud clear voice by an Etherian whom all the circle had come to know and trust:

"I have a body which is a duplicate of what I had on earth, the same hands, legs and feet and they move the same as yours do. This etheric body I had on earth interpenetrated the physical body. The etheric is the real body and an exact duplicate of our earth body. At death we just emerge from our flesh covering and continue our life in the etheric world, functioning by means of the etheric body just as we functioned on earth in the physical body. This etheric body is just as substantial to us now, as the physical body was to us when we lived on earth. We have the same sensations. When we touch an object we can feel it, when we look at something we can see it. Though our bodies are not material, as you understand the word, yet they have form and feature and expression. We move from place to place as you do, but much more quickly than you can."

Now that physical science has revealed to us that matter is an open net-work of vibrations, and that different frequencies (rate of recurrence of vibrations) can occupy the same space, it is possible to appreciate how two bodies can appear to us as one. The vibrations of one appeal to our sight and other senses, to be known as the physical body. The one which is not sensed on earth, and is invisible to us, we call the etheric body, which we will appreciate when it leaves the physical body under the control of our mind, the super-etheric picture maker which is our real selves.

So we once were told by one who has made the change called death:

"The spirit body (etheric body) has the same formation as the material body, and there is no one that has not a perfect spirit body. I have never seen anyone ailing or suffering in any way."

This was confirmed and enlarged upon on another occasion by one who had suffered much when on earth:

"Life with us is just wonderful, although I do not know much about it yet, dear. I have no pain now.

In this land of light and liberty pain does not exist. There is no pain now."

One of the most comprehensive statements concerning us as etheric beings was once given in these words:

"You are just as much an etheric being now as you will ever be. You are just as much in the etheric world now as you will ever be, only you do not appreciate the fact in consequence of your having a physical body attuned to physical surroundings. The etheric world is about and around you, and, at death, when you discard your physical body, you are in the etheric world without having to travel any distance to get there.

"You became immortal at your birth, and you are just as immortal now as you will ever be. Your physical body covers your etheric body, and you cannot appreciate your etheric body because it is made up of substance at a higher rate of vibration than your physical eye can see. When you die you will appreciate the etheric body, and cease to appreciate your physical body.

"Your new body grows more and more refined as time passes, and you will rise to higher and higher planes of consciousness. You will see more, and you will see further. You will hear more, and you will hear more clearly. Any deformities you have will be corrected here. If you have lost a leg or arm you will have it here, as it was only the physical arm or leg you lost."

A momentary pause and then the speaker continued his fluent remarks:

"Your understanding will be enlarged, and you

will be more conscious of the beauties of your surroundings than you are in the physical body. Your scope of usefulness will be extended beyond the limit of your present imagination. You will not have to trouble about money, about earning a livelihood, about eating or about clothes, or about a house to live in, as your mind will be in so much greater control of your surroundings that it will be able to mould those surroundings to meet your desires.

"There will be no more pain or sorrow or regret, no more grieving over separation after your loved ones from the earth have joined you. You will cease to regret the errors of the past through rectifying past mistakes. You will then enter on a life of eternal progress and everlasting blessedness."

To find oneself strong and well, in a body similar to the body which had been left on earth, must be a great surprise to most new arrivals in the other world. This is what we were once told:

"I wish I could portray to you the startled look on some of the faces of those who have made the change and find they are standing, firmly grounded. We try to explain to them that they have passed from the earth life into the Spirit World. As one young man, a young soldier, said to me: 'But I am myself; it is amazing—look—this is my hand; these are my legs; I am myself; I still have my body.' Then it dawns upon them, and immediately their thought is of those left behind whom they love. It may be a mother, sister, brother, wife or sweetheart. How to get into touch with them and let them know that everything is all right; that they still live. Their chief plaint is: 'Oh, that I could tell them.' We explain that this may be possible later on and then things are much better."

In answer to a question, we received the following reply:

"Yes, my heart functions—all our organs function, but not just as in the human body. I do not understand very well myself, but I like to be near when some of the beautiful shining and advanced ones come to talk to us and teach us. Do you know, I just plunk down and listen as earnestly as you would do yourselves."

As we are just mind, the wonderful substance which makes us conscious thinking individual beings, it consequently follows that memory does not die. We leave the physical body on earth to decay, but mind and the etheric body, being non physical, do not die or decay. So we find on our arrival in the etheric world that our memory of earth life is still with us, and we can recall the past as we did on earth.

Memory is our most wonderful possession, and the most potent argument in favour of our having a duplicate etheric body. Without memory we would be like dead things, and yet it is not physical in any sense. A man of seventy has not a single molecule present in his body which he had at the age of twenty. They have all been renewed, and yet his memory of events, his capacity to repicture past events right back to childhood, remains unimpaired, vivid, clear and distinct. Our memory goes with us when we die as it is part of our mind, and we find Etherians coming back and reminding us of things and events which happened in their childhood on earth.

It is not the food we eat which determines the shape and size of the physical body, as can be discovered by putting a foal or a calf or a lamb on a grass field. Though they eat the same food and drink the same water, yet the body of each develops differently in size and shape. Moreover, they are continually renewing their bodies. Throughout a lifetime the flesh and bones of humans and animals waste away completely, but we do not notice it because new flesh and bones take their place. Each physical cell is renewed, but how is this possible without a structure to support the physical cell in its decay and renewal?

To accept the reality of the etheric duplicate body for all living creatures, which our etheric friends tell us each one has, answers this problem. Consequently, it seems logical to accept what they tell us, because it fits in with what takes place on earth. If something permanent did not remain, our bodies would have no foundation or uniformity. So nature has provided this etheric structure from our conception, and during its earth life it clothes itself, sometimes imperfectly, with physical substance like a garment, which it casts aside when, as a perfect body, it enters the etheric world, its real home.

A man in Etheria who was blind on earth, when asked if he remembered someone he once knew, replied:

"Yes, I remember very well. I could not forget old friends. I am just waiting to see you all when you come over. I remember with joy many incidents in my earth life but God has given me a great blessing, Ladies and Gentlemen. He has given me eyesight that I may see and render a little service and succour to many of my fellow brothers and sisters in earth life when they come over here. I hope I did my little best while in earth life. It was very little but I did the best I could."

Blindness, deafness, and the other ills we suffer on earth pertain to the physical body. Consequently, our etheric eyes and hearing are perfect, because the etheric body is perfect. Those who were blind can once more see, those who had lost arms and legs on earth have them again, as it was the physical body which was damaged, not the etheric. I remember hearing the voice of a man who had lost an arm on earth exultantly telling me he now had both his arms.

My mother, who suffered much from rheumatism in her legs once said to me:

"I feel much younger now. I feel quite young again, no sore legs, and I can move about so freely. That has been my greatest satisfaction."

One who was deaf on earth once remarked:

"Sometimes my hearing was not good when I was in the body, but I can hear all right now."

Another said to a friend who was present:

"Well, I can get about now. Now that I have not the physical frame to hamper me. I was like you, and worse, for I was not half so active as you are, you know."

Another time we received this confirmation:

"When you come here, you find yourself possessed of a body—almost a replica of what you left behind, only younger-looking, though not immediately. I was resting, as I was told, for a considerable time when I first came over and, when this rest period was over, I found I had regained my lost youth, but, as I have already said, what troubled me was that I could not immediately go away with those I loved."

This Etherian who spoke was not prepared for a life more advanced than he could understand, but that would come later as he developed in understanding, wisdom, and knowledge.

Earth memories persist, as this old friend discovered:

"I have been some time in spirit life, and found it very difficult to be persuaded that I had finished with the old world. I found it difficult to realise that I had left the physical body behind when I found myself possessed of a body as real as the one I had had. One that I could travel with and could go and see people who were still in earth life, until I realised that they could not see me. I thought it was such a funny thing, and at first I found it difficult to be happy on the spirit side of life. It was a very hard struggle for me at first, but I ultimately came on someone who showed me the way whereby I could get into contact with those left behind, and from that time I made progress. I have not progressed very far, but I am now on the right way, and am happy."

Yes, they can travel far, and with ease in the etheric body. When once asked about this, the reply was emphatic:

"Certainly we move about in a body similar to the one we had on earth—similar in many ways, though not exactly the same. We walk, but there is another phase of it which I would like to explain to you. If we are tired—well, we do not tire here as you do—but if we feel we would like to go to a different place at a great distance, we just concentrate on that place and we are there instantly. There is a force whereby we can project ourselves to the desired destination, and visit these different colonies."

"Do you actually take your body with you?" someone asked.

"Yes, we are actually there in the body. When we have evolved sufficiently to live altogether on a higher plane, it is just a transition. When we acquire that power we go quite readily."

Our informants in Etheria consistently stated that there they do not grow old. Old age pertains to the physical body, but not to the etheric body. Consequently, those who pass on old on earth, with the disabilities of age, return to maturity in their etheric bodies, with the vitality and health which pertains to their new perfect bodies. Likewise, those who die young grow to maturity, remain in that condition, and never grow old.

On one occasion someone present complained of growing old, to be told by his wife from the other side:

"You have far too much of the 'old' to-day, Daddy, for I am getting younger all the time. You are maybe getting older, but inside yourself your spirit is renewing its youth, and you will find the benefit of it when the time comes for you to come over, and all you have loved here will help you."

This is what a mother in Etheria once told her daughter who was present at the séance. Someone had referred to growing old:

"You will never grow old, my dear, and, when

you come here, time will stand still for you, and you will never be old. You build the house which you will have on the spirit side of life by your actions on earth. I am not speaking to you individually now. I am speaking to you all, and when you cast aside the trammels of the earth life, and pass over, no matter how old you are, you come back to your youth again and your fullest vigour. There will be no forgetful memories in these days."

On another occasion, this lady was again told by her mother in Etheria:

"I have no halting walk now, Crissie, and I am never tired. It is so beautiful to walk about here. Life was getting rather difficult for me, Crissie, and all my trials are now over. Oh, it is Heaven at last—to be home."

Then, again, a son in Etheria told his mother on earth:

"You are not sad now, Mother, for you know I am not far from you. God bless you, my darling, my sweet Mother. I wish I could just let you see me. Well, you would say I had turned into a stalwart fine fellow now. You know, mothers never see any fault in their boys and they always praise them. I know I got praises when I did not deserve them, although I got a scolding now and again."

Once a grandfather told his granddaughter, who had called him "Grand-dad":

"You make me out a very old man when you say 'Grand-dad'. If you saw me now, you would be surprised. I always had a buoyant outlook. I was always a boy amongst boys, and, of course, a boy amongst the girls, amongst my own girls, I mean."

And another time a lady present heard this from her mother:

"You will get a big surprise when, in God's good time, you meet me again. You will not see a tottering old woman then, but one in the bloom of brightest youth coming to greet you. The halt, the maimed, the blind carry none of these infirmities to the land of spirit. If you are old on passing, you come back to the bloom of life, and if you are very, very young on coming to spirit life, you come to maturity, but you will know us all, and we never forget the dear ones that we left behind, and do all we can to help you on your journey."

In reply to a question I asked about the mind, I was told:

"Certainly your mind is something apart from the brain, you bring your mind over here with you. You leave your physical brain on earth. Our mind here acts on our etheric brain and through it on our etheric body, just as your physical brain acts on your physical body."

Consequently, as this is so, we can understand the following remarks made by a mother to her daughter on earth:

"I used to be forgetful, but I have a splendid memory now. I could puzzle you now."

To be repeated in other words on a later occasion:

"I know what it is to live in the past but you were always so good and kind to me. It is Mother."

Then, turning to another lady present, she addressed her by name:

"I could not memorise things very well, you

know. I forgot things and sometimes did stupid things, but Crissie was always kind."

Then, returning to her daughter, she said:

"That is what it was, Crissie, my memory just seemed to fade away, but you were always kind to me and helped me. God bless you. These kind deeds, my dear, are recorded. Don't you think anything about it. You will see your Mother on the other side of life in the full vigour of health, and memorising everything so well."

Here, something must be said about the colour of the etheric body. It is not black, white, yellow, or tan, as are our earth bodies, because the natural colouring of our skin comes about as the result of where we live on earth, the sun, or lack of sun, determining the colour of the skin of the bodies of the people on earth. So we need not be surprised to hear that the etheric body is not coloured like our physical body, but, instead, it radiates colours which are determined by our mental development.

Consequently a girl in Etheria, whose skin was black on earth, remarked that her body was black no longer, or, to put it in her own words:

"My skin was black in the old days, my heart is white now. I love you all. There is a shining light on your brows. I am not of any particular colour now. We lose the colours of the earth life as we come on, and we take on the vibrations and beauty of the spirit body which we have built for ourselves, and this makes us bright, or dull, as the case may be. I love colours and I try to make myself beautiful when I come to see you. I am not a black girl now. I did not like it. I am glad I am not."

From time to time during these séances, mention was made by the Etherians about the auras of the sitters. Our auras are the colours produced by the radiation of our etheric bodies, which can be seen by the people on the other side, though clairvoyants on earth also claim to be able to see them under suitable conditions. Ancient literature refers to the auras around certain people, and those who have studied the subject tell us that they change according to our emotions. The aura becomes red when we are angry, brown when we are avaricious, rose when affectionate, purple or blue when religious or devotional, green when deceitful or jealous, those having a normal yellow aura being intellectual. Our health also affects our auras, and the colour helps etheric doctors to diagnose a patient's condition on earth.

When we reach Etheria, the colours we radiate doubtless mean something different, but let us read what the Etherians had to say about the auras they saw radiating from the sitters at the Sloan circle.

On three separate occasions, three Etherian strangers came to our séance, being attracted by the auras emanating from the earth sitters. This is what one of them said:

"I know none of you, except by your auras which are round about you. They are very pleasing auras and indicate that you would be willing to give a helping hand to anyone who asked for help."

Another remarked:

"I do not know any of you personally. I was drawn here by the auras around you. I like the aura round about each and every one of you."

The third gave his name and said:

"I am Bob Hannah. I do not know any of you. I was just going round and thought I would come in when I saw the lights, the very bright lights, that surround you, to see if I could be of any help to any of you. I do not say that with any sense of exaltation, but I can see a wee bit further sometimes. I liked your auras and the conditions felt so harmonious that I just thought I would like to come in. I like the look of all of you. I saw so many lights dancing around you that I knew there were many friends, advanced friends, who were throwing their vibrations out to you."

The husband in Etheria of one of the sitters once spoke to a lady present. He often spoke to us, and this time he said:

"I see you have a clear perception of what the other side of life will open to you. Your life has been very clean and perfect. I do not speak in a flattering way, you know. I can see that outlook in the aura round about you."

When an Etherian was once asked to explain what he meant when he referred to a "shining one" he replied:

"An advanced spirit, who, having fulfilled the Master's Will, has acquired a degree of perfection to help others on their way upwards. He is a guide, so to speak, and his aura is of exceeding brightness. Everyone has an aura and some have such brilliant auras that it is almost impossible for some of us to gaze upon them."

"And what kind of aura has an Etherian who has not advanced far?" was once asked, to which the following reply was given:

"The aura of one who has not progressed far is not so clear and bright as the others, but the auras change as spiritual advancement develops, and those who are advancing gradually change in brightness as they endeavour to follow in the footsteps of the spirits ahead of them."

When one of the lady sitters was having a long talk with an Etherian, who knew and respected her son in Etheria, he added the following to his other interesting remarks:

"This is an experience which I appreciate very much, Mrs. Lang. I am watching the various phases which you are going through now, all of you in this little gathering, much of which is strange to me. I refer to the beautiful auras surrounding you."

Animal lovers will be pleased to know that their dead pets still live on. This is what I was once told when I asked if animals survive death:

"Most emphatically dogs, cats, and other animals survive death. No life becomes extinct, but they do not survive in the spirit world, as we term it. They have a spirit world of their own making. They do not exist in a spirit world as man exists. If, however, say a dog has affection for a human being, it can get into his or her surroundings if both have left earth."

This chapter comprises what has been told us by our friends in Etheria about the etheric body, and the aura it produces. Our mind, moreover, makes pictures of all we see and, by looking at it, they can see a picture of everything we see. They stand behind us, and to them our mind is like what a cinematograph technicolour picture is to us, all the objects and colours we see being seen by them. That is how they can read the book we are reading, as each page is pictured before them.

From time to time they spoke of the different parts of their own bodies, and, when these remarks are all brought together, it will be found that they referred to sixteen different parts, namely, their hands, fingers, face, lips, mouth, tongue, throat, legs, arms, feet, heart, head, hair, eyes, tears and internal organs, thus confirming that the etheric body is a duplicate of the physical body.

The next chapter will record what they had to say about the way they communicate with us.

CHAPTER V

COMMUNICATION

Anthropologists believe that the gift mankind has of being able to communicate his thoughts one to another has been one of the primary reasons for his great advance in intelligence beyond his animal ancestors. Spiritualists believe that the opening up of reliable communication between the so-called dead and the people of earth has been responsible for a religious revolution such as has never before been experienced. Communication between the two worlds is the foundation on which Spiritualism is built. On what we have been told by our friends who have passed on, Spiritualists have produced a natural religion, freed from the ignorance and superstition surrounding all the world's orthodox religions.

Just as speech between man and man on earth has raised us intellectually far above the beasts, so likewise has speech between the dead and the living raised Spiritualists intellectually above their contemporaries who continue to rely for their comfort and salvation on past tradition, lacking both truth and reason. This revolution in religious thought has come slowly but surely since the year 1848, the birth year of modern Spiritualism, as will be obvious to anyone who compares the barbaric and cruel religious beliefs prevalent in Christendom before that date with those preached to-day. In 1853 Dr. F. D. Maurice lost his professorship at King's College, London, because he cast doubt on hell being a fiery furnace. This is an instance of the then prevailing beliefs, but if we go back further we find multitudes being burned, hanged, imprisoned and banished, because their religious beliefs did not conform to those pronounced by an all powerful Church.

Mental development, the discoveries of science, and the knowledge we now have about our life after death, has made life on earth more tolerable for everyone, and relegated theology to the backwoods of ignorance and superstition. To-day science brings comfort and ease to all the advanced races of mankind, and Spiritualism tells us the truth about our future after death, and how we should live here to be happy hereafter.

Communication between this world and the next increases our mental development, because those who have gone on before come back to tell us what is true and what is not true in past religious teaching. Instead of being trained from childhood to believe the impossible, we are now told by our friends in Etheria that they have discovered how mistaken their religious teaching was on earth, and how we should avoid it for ourselves and our children. It is what you are that is important, and, though faith and belief may help as a crutch throughout our earthly pilgrimage, yet the place we reach in Etheria will be decided by ourselves by our own mental development. So we are told that each of us should do our best on earth, and if we do that we can do no better.

This chapter is devoted to the methods used by Etherians to communicate with us. We supply the mediums, but it is they who make communication possible, so let us read what they have to tell us. There are four ways in which this is done, by direct voice, trance, clairaudience and automatic writing. They can indicate their presence in other ways, but the foregoing are their principal means of communication. Much the best way is by what is called the Direct Voice, when they use their own voices and so cut out the mind of the medium, which, consequently, does not influence their conversations. We much prefer direct speech on earth to having everything we hear come through an intermediary. Likewise, to hear their own voices makes conversation much more interesting, reliable and satisfactory, because the medium's mind does not distort what they say as it may do when other methods are used.

All the extracts of conversations recorded in this book, except one, were spoken by Etherians by means of the Direct Voice. The one exception was when the medium was in trance, and this fact is mentioned when it occurs. This makes this collection unique and much more valuable than those records made up of trance utterances, or automatic writing and clairaudience. Moreover, they tell us the methods they employ to make communication possible, and first of all we shall consider what they have to say about the production of the Direct Voice.

When I set about making my enquiry, the place in space from which the voices came was uppermost in my mind. So I put this question to an Etherian with whom I was speaking: "You told me your world revolved with this world. How does this happen, and also, do you travel with the earth round the sun?"

This was his reply:

"The spheres nearest the earth revolve because we belong to this planet. We cannot see your world revolving in space, because we revolve with you. We cannot see your world until we take on earth conditions. In taking these on, we slow down our vibrations, and come through from one plane to another, until we get our vibrations down more to a level with those of which your world is composed. We can all come down, but we cannot go up beyond our own plane until we are prepared for the change."

On this occasion I was alone with the medium, except for my secretary, who was at a table on the other side of the room taking notes in shorthand of everything I said, and everything said by the various voices which spoke that evening. Taking shorthand notes in the dark is quite possible by an expert stenographer.

I had carefully searched the small room in which this séance was held, made sure that the window was tightly shut and that the door was locked, the key being in my pocket. Then I took my seat opposite the medium, and when a voice spoke I leaned forward and put my ear close to his mouth, but nothing but his steady quiet breathing could be heard, whereas the different voices which spoke could be heard from all parts of the room.

They were loud and clear and, if the medium had been speaking, I would have heard him even if it had been a form of ventriloquism. A ventriloquist speaks the words without seemingly moving his lips and, by making a dummy move its lips, deludes people into thinking that the words are being spoken by the dummy. This deception is only possible in daylight, but not in the dark, and no one can practice it without using his own vocal organs.

The medium sat still on his chair throughout the séance, as I had my left foot over and touching his right foot, and my right foot over and touching his left foot, but his feet remained still throughout. My left hand held his right hand and my right hand held his left hand throughout the séance. Nevertheless, bright lights floated about the room. On other occasions when my hands were free I tried to catch them, but could not, as they always evaded me, which was proof that they were guided by intelligences which could see in the dark These lights were seen at all the séances recorded in this book.

After thirty-nine séances I had with John Sloan, for which he refused any payment, I was satisfied, after applying every test I could think of, that the voices were not those of the medium or anyother earth person present. Moreover, those who spoke could see in the dark, as whenever we asked the time it was correctly told. If someone had a luminous watch it was put away in a pocket or handbag, when the séance commenced, to be consulted only after the time was told. The two trumpets of about two feet high, which were in the centre of the circle of sitters when the séance commenced, floated about all over the room as high as the ceiling, sometimes at great speed, and could be seen when they were coated with a band of luminous paint. The hands of the medium, and of each sitter in the circle, were held from start to finish.

On another occasion, I asked for an explanation as to how it was possible for our atmosphere to be vibrated to enable us to hear the words they spoke, and this was the answer I received:

"I speak by materialising my etheric mouth and tongue. I shall do my best to make you understand how this is done, but remember you cannot get a proper grasp of the difficulties we are faced with until you yourself come across to our side. However, I shall explain our methods as clearly as possible. From the medium, and those present, a chemist in the etheric world withdraws certain ingredients which, for want of a better name, is called ectoplasm. To this the chemist adds ingredients of his own making. When these are mixed together a substance is formed which enables the chemist to materialise his hands. He then, with his materialised hands, constructs a mask resembling the mouth and tongue.

"The spirit wishing to speak places his face into this mask and finds it clings to him, it gathers round his mouth, tongue and throat. At first, difficulty is experienced in moving this heavier material, but by practice this becomes easy. The etheric organs have once again become clothed in matter resembling physical matter, and, by the passage of air through them, your atmosphere can be vibrated, and you hear his voice."

This means that the basic substance needed for the production of the Direct Voice is Ectoplasm. It might be called the connecting link between the physical and the etheric, as it is the substance supplied by our body which, when mixed with etheric ingredients, can be handled by Etherians. It is the thing which is half-way between physical and etheric substance, and it acts as a bridge between the two worlds. Those rare men and women, called Direct Voice mediums, have this ectoplasm in much greater abundance than the rest of us, as we all have it in a lesser degree, and this being so their presence is necessary before the Direct Voice can be produced from Etheria.

So intrigued was J. Gilbert E. Wright, an American Research chemist, with this elusive stuff, that he set about making a study of it, to end in setting down ninety-six different observations on its effects and behaviour, but only the most important will here be mentioned.

When under the influence of Etheric chemists, the medium's body is used as a supply basis for the ectoplasm, and they take what they can from the sitters, but under normal conditions it cannot be seen or tasted and it gives off no smell.

This stuff seems to diffuse through the tissues of the body like a gas, and emerges through the orifices because it passes more freely through mucous membrane than through the skin, to become, by treatment from etheric chemists, an amorphous (shapeless) viscous (sticky) liquid which can be seen at times in red light. It has now some of the properties of matter, as it occupies space and can be seen. Its weight is difficult to determine, but, if the medium and sitters sit on weighing-machines during the séance, their weight will decrease, especially that of the medium, to become normal when the sitting is over. This has been proved by experiment.

Now to continue my questions and the answers I received.

"I have often heard two, or sometimes three, voices speak at once. Are other masks used in these circumstances?" I asked, to receive the following reply:

"Yes, on these occasions conditions are good, and the chemist has sufficient ectoplasm to construct several masks, which are all sometimes used at the same time. That accounts for your hearing more than one voice speaking."

"Where is the mask placed?" was my next question, to which I received the following answer:

"Usually, the mask is placed in the centre of the circle. The chemist keeps as much ectoplasm as possible within the circle, but, when the quantity given off by the medium and sitters is small, it gathers about the floor which accounts for voices coming from the floor when conditions are poor. On the other hand, when conditions are good and we have an ample supply, we can build right up to the ceiling, which accounts for the voices on these occasions coming from high up in the room.

"The person wishing to speak takes up his position in the centre of the circle, and presses into the ectoplasmic materialisation and then commences to speak, moving his mouth and tongue just as you do when you speak.

"The trumpet is used, not only to magnify the voice, but to enable it to be directed towards the person we wish to speak to. The trumpet is moved by materialised rods, and is controlled by one on this side whom we term the trumpet operator."

The Etherian who said this now remarked that his co-worker, named Gallacher, would now speak. I thanked him for what he had told me, and then a new voice spoke to me with a strong Irish brogue. I expressed my pleasure in hearing him speak, and my regret that I was not able to see him. Then I asked him to tell me what he and the other helpers on his side did to make it possible for him and others to speak to me.

This was his reply:

"When a spirit wishes to speak to you he takes on earth conditions from your surroundings. We always know when your meetings take place. I am responsible for manipulating the trumpet. I have been standing beside you waiting to speak to you, and I am glad of the chance to tell you what I can.

"When there is going to be a meeting, the chemist whom I work with generally lets me know when it is going to occur, and asks me to come along at the specified time. He supplies a substance, and also obtains a certain amount from the medium and the other sitters. It is the combination of this spirit-substance with ectoplasm, drawn from the medium and sitters, which enables us to materialise. If there is enough it allows the metallic instrument to go to all parts of the room, and voices to be produced.

"When I came here tonight I first looked to see where I could best gather the most ectoplasm. The chemist gets it from me and adds his ingredients, and it is then conveyed to the most suitable place. I also speak for those who cannot do so, and also for those who may be a long distance away. These latter send me their messages as you send messages by wireless; these are picked up by a receiver and given to me ; I then pass them on, giving the person's name. I merely act as an Exchange.

"When spirits come into the circle to speak they actually, for the time being, partially materialise ; their mouth and tongue being coated by the substance we make. There is a nexus between the medium's larynx and the materialised mouth and tongue of the spirit speaking, which enables the words the speaker forms to be heard by you. We then feel as we did when on earth. The organs of speech take on a thicker form, our tongue thickens and so do all the other materialised organs.

"We cannot be heard by you until we again put on matter of slower vibration, and it is only when we find someone like the medium, who can supply us with this ectoplasm, which we fashion to our requirements, that we can again make you hear us. Ectoplasm alone, however, would be of no use without the chemical substance we supply from our side. It would not materialise without it."

"What is this substance?" I asked.

"The chemist is standing beside me, and tells me to say it is no use giving you its ingredients as they would mean nothing to you on earth. He says, however, that the finished product is a substance by which material things can be moved. Nothing can be moved without it. All physical bodies are composed of many different ingredients from which we draw the substance you call ectoplasm."

"Can you tell me something more about the mask which you enter when you speak to us?"

"You can call it a mask or a dummy. We gather the ectoplasm from the sitters into what I might term an urn; not a physical urn. If you wait a moment I shall try and show you it. (Sloan's hands and feet were still controlled. I waited, and gradually there appeared high above his head a luminous object which assumed the shape of a large flower-pot, and then faded away.) Did you see it? (Yes, I replied.) Well, we gather the ectoplasm into this, and the chemist adds his ingredients. The finished product is matter slow enough in vibration to vibrate your atmosphere. The mask, until it is entered by the spirit wishing to speak, is incapable of speaking itself. The spirit has to tune down his organs of speech, and thus contact between these and the mask becomes established. When the magnetic or psychic power is strong enough, there is no difficulty in obtaining sufficient cohesion between the speaker's organs and the mask. When cohesion is established, the ectoplasmic material moves with the vocal organs of the spirit. It is exactly as if we coated our mouth and tongue with this material. It sticks to them and moves with them."

"Has the mask weight; would it affect a balance?" I asked.

"Yes, the mask has weight. The ectoplasm taken from the sitters has weight, and the sitters' weight is reduced in proportion to the amount that is withdrawn. If you were to sit on a weighing-machine during the sitting you would find your weight decrease. The ectoplasm is returned to the sitters at the end of the séance and they become normal."

This statement, as mentioned some pages back, has been proved to be correct by careful experiment with the sitters in the circle sitting on weighing-machines.

Once I asked what they meant when they spoke about taking on earth conditions before they were able to speak to us, and this is what I was told:

"We lower our vibrations when we speak to you, that is what we mean when we say we take on earth conditions."

I asked what was meant by the expression, "We lower our vibrations", to which enquiry came the answer:

"It is difficult to explain how it is we lower our vibrations. It is a condition you get yourself into, which enables you to absorb the ectoplasm from the medium and sitters, and when I do so I feel just as I did when I lived on earth."

"And does that also explain how you hear us?" I asked, to which question the Etherian replied:

"We hear you speak by lowering our vibrations sufficiently to catch the atmospheric vibrations of your voice."

When he finished speaking, a new loud clear voice said that he would answer any further questions I had to ask. So I said, "You go on talking. You may say something I have not heard before," and this is what I heard:

"I feel as if I were just back on earth again. This is just as interesting to me as it would be for you to come over here to our side and see how this is worked. You would be fascinated seeing all that takes place before a spirit voice can vibrate your atmosphere. First we are told by Whitefeather, or someone else, when a séance is to take place; he is always about the medium and knows everything he does, and hears when he arranges a séance. Then we all come. Whitefeather gets the spirit-body out of the medium's body, the chemist and his assistants come with their preparations, and Gallacher comes to manage the trumpets—not that the trumpets are always necessary; you have often heard us speak without them. They just magnify the voice and enable us to throw it more easily to the person we wish to speak to.

"Greentree then takes charge and tells the spirits present how and when to speak. It is very interesting watching all the arrangements being made on this side, the chemist linking up the medium and sitters and drawing power from them. Until all these preparations are completed no voice can be produced that you could hear. The larger end of the megaphone or trumpet is also used to place the materialised mouth and tongue in, as it gives the spirit speaking something to rest them on. Then we speak, pointing the smaller end to the person addressed."

"How is it you move the trumpets?" I now asked, to receive this reply:

"When the power is strong enough, the spirit's hand is sufficiently materialised to move the trumpet and enable him to hold it, but on other occasions it is moved by psychic rods."

At another séance an Etherian had difficulty at first in being heard, but when his voice became strong and clear he volunteered this information:

"I had trouble before I got the vibration to-day, but now I have it all right. I will speak in terms understandable to all. You know what the wireless is? Well, if you go just the slightest degree off the station, there is a blur and you do not get the message. We are working on a theory like that. We must get the exact vibration before we can get a message through."

At the end of a sitting the voices as a rule become weaker, because the ectoplasm from the medium and sitters has been used up. Once, just as a long séance was coming to a close, the following explanation was given to account for the voices being weaker, and the séance being brought to a close:

"The power which has been in your surroundings of late has dispersed very much and I would not advise you to continue too long, because I could not control so many on this side who want to come and speak to you, and it might be immature to let them in just yet. I am glad you understand. Just close in the ordinary way, and we will say our blessing and our benediction on you from this side, so that it may follow you when you go hence. God bless you."

On another occasion the same reason was given for bringing the séance to a close:

"And now I think it is about time to stop. There has been a great deal taken out of you dear people to-day, unknown to you, and there are some of you not just in the best condition to be sapped. However, you must judge for yourselves if you have been long enough. Do not consider us for we are at your service to do what we can."

The same information was given us towards the end of another séance:

"Now the day is far spent. I am not speaking about wearying to get away, but we just thought that perhaps there had been enough drawn out of you, because you know that while you are sitting here in a Meeting, I don't know what you call it, communion with the people whom you loved in earth life and who have been promoted to our side of life, you lose a lot of the substance of your physical energy. Sometimes we manage to give it back to you again, but sometimes we fail to do so. It is not by our will, but our inability to complete that which we would like to complete, in returning to you what has been taken. You will never, however, be injured in any way."

The mother of a lady who was present once had an intimate conversation with her daughter, who remarked that her mother's voice was different from what she remembered it to be. When we consider the difficult conditions under which they speak, with their vocal organs covered by a mask of ectoplasmic stuff, this change in the tone of the voice can be understood. The mother replied to her daughter in these words:

"Janie, it is very difficult for us to get our voices just as you knew them in earth life. I am still beside you, darling."

One who said he was a Scottish Highlander when on earth, once remarked on this difficulty:

"It was the earnest thoughts of those of you who are anxious about loved ones who are out of your ken at present that made me so anxious to speak, and I thought if I could bring just a little ray of hope, a little ray of comfort, and a little word of love to you, I would be doing something in the Master's service. God bless you all. I do not find my voice as clear as I would like it to be, but, when we come near the surroundings of the Earth Plane, we have to use the vibrations which are round about, and it may be impossible to attune our voices into the tone that you think unmistakable."

This concludes what I have been told about the methods they use to communicate with us on earth by means of the Direct Voice, when they speak direct to us with their own vocal organs. Another method is by taking control of the medium. Then they separate his etheric body from his physical body, and when this takes place we say he is in trance. Before the trance state comes on, the medium becomes passive and quiet, as one does before going to sleep, but instead of quietly sleeping he speaks in a voice unlike his own. Now he is what is called "controlled", as the usual characteristics of the individual are absent, his personality, his mannerisms, his sense of feeling pain, and his memory have gone, to be replaced by an entirely new unseen personality who carries on a conversation with the sitters.

In the case of Sloan, before the new personality spoke a singular phenomenon took place. A bluish light crossed the room obliquely and approached Sloan. When it reached him, his mouth spoke, but not in his own voice. His control, Whitefeather, spoke, and announced that he was now in control of the medium. The shape of this light was sometimes round, or semi-circular, or oblong, six to eight inches across, and was seen by everyone present, but not at Sloan's séances only.

It has been seen at other séances, and is referred to in ancient literature, the best known passages being the record of the Spirit of God descending like a dove and alighting upon Jesus. The other is the account of tongues like as of fire, which alighted on the disciples when they were filled with the Holy Ghost at the séance they held on the Day of Pentecost. (The correct translation of Holy Ghost is "Divine Spirit", the name the early followers of Jesus gave to the medium's spirit control.) Like Sloan, each disciple then began to speak in a voice other than his own.

When the control left Sloan the blue light likewise left him as it had come, floating out of sight, and it was always referred to as "Whitefeather's light".

When Sloan was controlled they used a different procedure to that adopted to produce the Direct Voice, which often took place when he was normal, and this is what I was told was the way they made use of Sloan's vocal organs when he was in trance.

"When I control the medium, I take on earth conditions, slow down my vibrations and stand behind him. Ectoplasm is found everywhere in the human body. When I stand behind him it is similar to standing behind the mask, only in this case it is the medium's own vocal organs which I move to form the words; they move in company with my organs, whereas, when we speak directly apart from the medium, we enter the mask and form the words by our tongues which are temporarily materialised."

"When you control the medium and use his vocal organs, what really happens?" I now asked.

"When the medium is controlled, and we wish to speak through his vocal organs, we get him into a passive condition. This is the condition he is in when in trance. His spirit has left his body for the time being, and is outside. When he is in this condition we are able to work on his larynx and vocal cords, his tongue and throat muscles. We do not go inside him, however, but stand behind him. We are able to get ourselves into a condition, or in tune with the medium, to such an extent that when we move our voice organs the medium's move likewise.

"There is a connecting link, etheric or psychic, whichever you like to call it, which has the same action on the medium's muscles as a tuning fork on another tuning fork if they are both tuned to the same pitch. Thus the two sets of vocal organs work in harmony. There is no question of the messages in any way being influenced by the medium's mind, as his mind does not come into the question at all. We do not work through his mind, but directly on his vocal organs. Everything that comes through is exactly as it originates in the mind of the controlling spirit. The medium's mind and brain are switched off for the time being, and the spirit operator controls the muscles of the medium's vocal organs."

On one occasion, when the medium was in trance, I asked, "Where has his spirit been since we started?", to be told by the Etherian to whom I was speaking:

"When the trance state comes on it means that the medium's spirit has moved out of his body. His spirit is at present exactly on his right not far from his body."

At another séance I asked for an explanation of the difference between trance and sleep, and this is what I was told. It was the only occasion, to my knowledge, when a record was made of anything said through Sloan in trance:

"In sleep—that is, natural sleep, the sleep the physical body needs—all the functions of the body are at rest except the heart, which keeps on pulsating. That is natural sleep, but the spirit does not always leave the body. In trance we put the spirit slightly aside, but a psychic cord is attached to his body from his spirit-body. If that cord should be snapped, dissolution would take place immediately. Before we can speak through him we require to get his spirit out of him, outside altogether, but it is still attached to the body by this cord of life. He is now unconscious and outside his physical body. His spirit at the moment is exactly between his body and you. If nothing untoward happens he can return to his body just as he left it. If something should go wrong in his present condition, the physical frame suffers. On this occasion you will notice I am speaking to you by means of his vocal organs. I am standing behind him, but am in such close contact with these organs that, just as I move my mouth, his mouth moves. I am in complete control of these organs. The medium knows nothing, he is quite unconscious of anything I do. I am taking temporary use of his body, as the power is not yet strong enough to speak to you by the Direct Voice."

"How does the medium hear clairaudiently?" I asked.

"The medium hears clairaudiently by our acting on his mind."

A gentleman present was spoken to once by his uncle who gave his name. In the course of conversation his uncle remarked:

"I think once upon a time you did not think there was much in this. I used to sense that feeling, but, my word, you know now that it is true enough. It was a boon to me and to your aunt when we lost our boy. I thought the world was finished when he went, but we are happy now, and together."

At another séance a husband in Etheria had a long and evidential conversation with his wife who was present. At its close a gentleman in the circle asked him if many in Etheria knew of this way of communicating with their friends on earth. This was the reply:

"Mr. Cameron, there are myriads here who do not know about this means of communication at all. I did not know much about it for a time on your side until I lost my boy, and my boy, Eleanor (turning to his wife), you know what he meant to me, and that day at Mrs. Motion's when I first heard my boy speaking to me, the world opened afresh. For all that I owe thanks to my dear old friend Daddy Sloan."

An Etherian, who had just finished telling his sister, who was present, that the knowledge that he and she would meet again made life worth living, then turned to an army officer, who was one of the circle, and said:

"Captain Altree, I am sure you understand that as well. The knowledge that those whom we have loved in earth life can come back and touch you and talk to you is a great boon indeed, and a great blessing, is it not?"

Once the following was said to a lady present by a relation on the other side:

"Your minds are so much taken up with other things, that it is difficult to keep in touch with you all, and there are so many stragglers near your world just now, who are desperately endeavouring to get into touch with any channel through which they can communicate with those they love, to tell them that they are not dead. They wish to tell those that they have left behind that they are alive and not dead, living a freer and a fuller life, free from the trammels of the earth body, living in purer air, a purer atmosphere, and purer surroundings. We are trying our best to bring back with us an element of that purity to strengthen your souls in the struggle of life, in the struggle that is still before you."

Not once, but many times we were told of the anxiety of those who have recently passed over to come back and tell their friends on earth that they are alive and not dead. This is what was told us by one who was a regular communicator:

"Many are near the Earth Plane, who see the lights round about you and are desperately anxious to get in touch. It is the kind thoughts coming from a gathering such as this that brings them. They are sure to return again. It is a doorway which they can come to, to try and get into contact with those they love in earth life."

The same theme was touched on at another séance, the Etherian speaking regarding communication from the point of view of the people on earth:

"It means something in life, you know, and it will be something in the life on my side when you come here, to know that you have been the recipient of messages given to you from time to time, which you have in turn handed on to others, and which will help them along the road of life. There are many friends on the Earth Plane, who have not had the opportunities that you and some of the others present may have had to gain a knowledge of this truth, and your experience will be a blessing to others."

We do not lose our memory of earth life when we pass on, as a grandmother once told her granddaughter who was present.

"It is a funny, funny thing, the memories that cling to us when we come back amongst people like you. It brings back to our memories the lovely days that have passed into the shade a little."

It is not allowed by those in charge of the séance on the other side, that everything they know about us be spoken about by them at a séance. A certain amount of tact is necessary, as they know what we think, and that we do things which we do not wish spoken about. They can read the pictures our minds make, and see the things we do. So they try to say nothing to annoy or embarrass us. Addressing a lady present on one occasion, an Etherian said:

"God bless you, and protect you now at this time. I think you know what I mean. Of course, little lady, there are things which I would not tell you of before others, and there are things which belong to Mr. Cameron himself, just as there are things which belong to you—you understand. It is meant for the spirit recess of his own soul, to help him to press onward towards the mark of the high calling, which is beyond the vale and the shadow of tears."

The same topic was dealt with at another séance. In reply to a question, we received this reply:

"I am not permitted to say. You will find some funny reasons when you come to my side, my friends. There is a sort of censorship, if you understand what I mean, but we are all brothers and sisters on this side, willing to help each other in every way possible."

A sitter once passed the remark that some day communication with the other side will be taken for granted, just as so many things once thought impossible are now accepted as a matter of course. To this opinion an Etherian replied:

"Hear, hear! It is just coming to that. We will pop in, in the night, and talk to you and go away again, and it will all be considered quite normal. All of you just do your best to spread this truth, no matter how hard it may be, just a kindly word, a kindly thought, a good aspiration, or kind deeds. All these things help."

I once asked if they kept records on their side, of what took place at our séances, to which I received the reply:

"Yes, of course we keep records of what takes place. We are not encyclopedic."

During these séances the Etherians made their presence known in other ways than by talking. The two trumpets were moving about the room much of the time, sometimes beating on the ceiling. When not being spoken through they would touch different sitters at times, and stroke their hands or faces. As I have already said, bright lights the size of half-a-crown moved about the room, but could never be caught.

Materialised fingers and hands stroked the hands and faces of the sitters, or were felt in one's hair, but never did they annoy anyone.

Several times I thought of something and asked what I was thinking about. Immediately a voice spoke to me and told me correctly what it was. I was told that when we think, our mind makes pictures to which we give the name of "thoughts". Our thoughts are the mental pictures made by that highly plastic substance termed "mind stuff", at a high frequency of vibration, much higher than the frequency of our etheric body. Our mind is constantly moulding itself into pictures, and when we sleep we notice them, calling them dreams. In sleep they are not controlled as they are when we are awake, but, whether controlled or not, they make up our life and, as our mind pictures, so we are, so is our character, our mental development and our happiness.

These séances lasted from two to three hours. None of us was in any way adversely affected physically by them, but those who were mediumistic did feel exhausted. Sloan soon recovered his strength, but one man I knew sometimes took an hour or so before his normal strength returned. He always lost a considerable amount of ectoplasm during a séance, and it seemed as if he recovered it more slowly than did the medium and the rest of us.

This chapter concludes the first part of this book, and it is intended as an introduction to Part Two. We have read that a medium is necessary before we can hear the voices, because he supplies most of the ectoplasm which the Etherians require before they can materialise their vocal organs. We have read about the two stenographers who took accurate notes of everything said at the séances. We have learned about our etheric body. This is vital knowledge, as without this understanding we cannot comprehend how we can survive without our physical body. Neither can we understand how it is possible for communication to take place between the two worlds. Without a body speech is impossible.

In this chapter we have learned how speech between the visible and invisible world is not only possible but actually happens, and now we shall leave this world of physical matter and learn what takes place when we die. Then we shall read about the world we shall some day inhabit, what its inhabitants are like, and what they think.

The extracts given in this book are taken from conversations which were restricted in their scope, because they took place between people who were separated in place and thought, the Etherians being in one order of existence and we in another. Except for their memories of earth life, and their interest in, and affection for, those they knew who were still on earth the affairs of this world have been left behind for ever. Moreover, so far as their present life is concerned, as we have not experienced it, they could only speak about it in a general way and in language we could understand.

It is very important that we remember the reason for the limited scope of their power to converse with us, but, if we always keep this in mind, we can now pass on to the next phase of our enquiry into the Greater World, a place that is very real to its inhabitants, though unreal to us while in the physical body.

PART TWO

CHAPTER VI

THE PASSING OVER

THE small gathering of men and women, about ten in all, were seated in a circle with two aluminium trumpets, each of somewhat over two feet high, placed in the centre. We were in darkness; conversation had been general, to be followed by a hymn to create greater harmony and vibrate the atmosphere. This helped those who were present from the other side to gather the ectoplasm from the medium and sitters, without which no voices could be heard.

After the hymn was sung there was silence. All waited expectantly. The note-taker sat prepared, with her notebook and pencil, to record the voices when they spoke. Then, out of the silence, came a man's voice which spoke to someone present, to be answered just as we do in ordinary conversation. The voice gave the name of the speaker, who addressed by name the person on earth spoken to, and, when he had finished, another voice spoke to someone else, to be likewise answered. Intimate and evidential details were given to make recognition possible. Thus the strange conversations went on, men, women and children of the other world, who had materialised their vocal organs so as to vibrate our atmosphere, conversing with their friends who had gathered together in a small room of a house in Glasgow.

Once again came a short silence, to be broken by a woman's voice which all recognised. She had passed on a few years previously and she had spoken often before, clearly and easily, because she was acquainted with the conditions, having been a regular member of the circle before she had parted from us. She always addressed her husband as "Daddy", and, as he was present, this is what we all heard her say to him:

"Dear Daddy, when you took my poor old finished remains to the cemetery, I wished you had not come, for I was not there at all. Of course, you knew that."

No, she was not there, but it is so natural to look upon the physical body as the person, because it is only that part of us which appeals to our physical senses. The part that does not influence our senses, the invisible part, we do not appreciate. The invisible part of us leaves the physical body at death, to start a new life in a different environment which is vibrating at a frequency in harmony with the duplicate etheric body.

Consequently, the individual, who has parted from his physical body, finds himself in a body like the one he has just left, and in a world he can appreciate. His mind can now respond to the higher vibrations, because it has a vehicle which is in harmony with its new surroundings, just as we in the physical body respond to our physical environment during earth life. So, except for a new body, we are the same in looks and character as we were on earth, no better and no worse.

Now this woman came back to tell her bereaved

husband and her friends that, though lost to sight, she was the same person as she was before she had left her earth body.

On another occasion when a sitter referred to a young woman who had passed over, a voice, giving name and correctly claiming to be that of her Minister when on earth, loudly exclaimed:

"Yes, but you did not see the beautiful soul that left the bodily casket, a soul full of purity and love. She comes back and speaks to you at times."

What much distresses our friends who have passed on is the fact that so many on earth think of them as lying in their graves. Those on the other side who know that communication is possible with earth, and their number is small, try as soon as possible after arrival to tell their friends on earth that they are not dead, but very much alive. This being so, we can appreciate the thoughts uppermost in the mind of a young boy who once returned to speak to his mother who was present. He gave his name, and this is what he said about himself and his father who had also passed on:

"Be glad for us that we are over here, we are not dead you know."

"I know that, Bobby dear," the mother replied, and he continued:

"Yes, but don't ever think of us lying up in West Kilbride behind the dyke yonder. I have never been there, Mother dear. I am living in your heart and in your memory, and, when the shadows have departed and the mists have rolled away, then we will greet you here. I have so much to show you, so much to tell you, dear Mother."

On another occasion, the following assurance was given:

"It is only a step over here, and you will have no difficulty in finding the door. We will be watching, and loving hands will welcome you on the shore. You know we love you and will always stand by you."

This, then, is the first step we all must take on our journey through the spheres. We discard the old body which has done its work, and live on in our etheric duplicate body which has always interpenetrated our physical body, and been the structure on which the material has grown and developed.

The etheric body is not just an inference or an hypothesis, as it has been seen by clairvoyants from time to time when leaving the body at death. This is how the famous medium Hudson Tuttle clairvoyantly witnessed a death. In his own words he tells us that:

"Slowly the spiritual form (spiritual body) withdrew from the extremities and concentrated in the brain. As it did so, a halo arose from the crown of the head which gradually increased. Soon it became clear and distinct, and I observed that it had the exact resemblance of the form it had left. Higher and higher it arose, until the beautiful spirit stood before us and the dead body reclined below. A slight cord connected the two, which, gradually diminishing, became in a few minutes absorbed and the spirit had forever quitted its earthly temple."

Under the guidance of our mind, which controls the new body as it did the old, we pass out of our earth body by the top of the head, to arrive, when the short cord between the two bodies is broken, in a new environment. Our old surroundings have passed away, we sense them no more and a new life opens before us. What it will mean to us will be told in the next chapter. This experience has come to all who have lived on earth, it will come to all who now live on earth, and to all who will live here in the years to come.

This we know because the voice of one who had made the change once told those present:

"Death is not the end but the beginning. I think it is a triumphal march when you leave the physical, if your life has been spent in the way in which you ought to have spent it. If this is so, it is a triumphal march to the spirit side of life, which is a path of glory all the way. It is for you I am speaking and for myself as I was hitherto. When you realise before passing on that you have your duty to do in the earth life, and, provided you do it, you will pass on to a more bright and glorious way of life. It was like this I did the triumphal march across the border. I hope that will be your portion when your time comes. Do you know there is no balancing of accounts here? They are all balanced before you come, and also the path is clearly laid out, the path by which you have come and also the path by which you should have come. I am sorry to say I did not always walk in the right path."

The voice which spoke these words claimed to come from a man who was in his time a well-known banker in Glasgow, and one who had been looked upon with much esteem. He gave his name and earth address to a gentleman present whom he had known well on earth, and spoke to him about things they had done together. His words came clearly and precisely without hesitation, just as did those of the many men, women, and children whose words are recorded in this book.

On one occasion came the voice of one who claimed to have been a clergyman on earth. He gave his name and earth address, and this is what he said:

"For those who have lost, or think they have lost, dear ones, may they acquire knowledge such as you have, of knowing that their dear ones have just passed the borderline of life, and gone to a far happier world. God bless you, and now may the peace and the blessing, the fellowship and communion of those in spirit life be permitted to come and mingle with those on earth, cheering them and bearing them up on their way through life, until they, too, shall pass onwards to better things."

When a question was once asked about the location of the etheric world, the following trite reply was given:

"Don't you bother about where the Spirit World is, you will be there all right when the time comes, the whole lot of you. What I would like to tell you is to prepare yourself on your side of life, so that you will be fitted and able to take a reasonable place and a reasonable responsibility on the spirit side when you do come over."

Always the stress is laid on our own personal responsibility, and that on earth we are preparing our place hereafter. It is now that we are making our future conditions.

"Do we remember our earth life?" someone once asked, to receive this reply:

"To a certain extent you remember everything when you pass on, but things which happened in the body, and are not to your benefit on the spirit side, gradually fade away."

What then will be our last experience on earth? This was told to a lady on another occasion by her grandfather, but he did not say that it happened to everyone:

"All the lovely scenes of the past that you have forgotten, scenes in your earth life, will pass before you like a panoramic vision and bring it all back again. It is often revealed to those that are just passing, at the last moment. I am sure you will have heard from those about you that one who had died was speaking of old scenes just before he passed away. That was just a panoramic vision passing before him. God bless you, my dear."

After passing over, all pain and illness are left behind. The regret comes from the separation from those left on earth, but the new arrival is met by friends who have already made the change. To them, what has taken place is the cause of rejoicing, because what causes sorrow on earth gives pleasure in Etheria.

This is what a lady present was once told:

"There is no dividing line between the hearts which beat in harmony and love, and the passing of one from the physical side to the spiritual side of life does not sever them. Yes, there is no dividing line at all. Those that you have loved best, little lady, those that are nearest to your heart—I mean your earth life heart—will be the ones who will come very near to you when you pass over, and you will know them, no matter how long they have been over."

Death, or reaching the etheric world, is not the crossing of wide spaces, as we have always been in that world, though we knew it not. Death is a change in the appreciation of the vibrations in which we live. It is like switching from one programme on the radio to another. Our etheric body responds to a higher frequency of the vibrations which are all around us, and consequently, when we pass on, we, at first, are in the same place as we were when we were alive on earth.

Then, with consciousness and health returned, we rise to the plane for which we are fitted, but our surroundings at first are so alike this earth that some find it difficult to appreciate that they have passed from earth, until they meet their friends who had made the change before them. Thus, they come to realise the fact that death is an experience which no one need fear, as it is painless and like going to sleep, to awaken in a new body in a beautiful country where their friends are waiting to welcome them. We all will have a wonderful experience some day, but it is only the few who know it.

Until we understand what death is, we cannot understand what life is, and this profound thought will be appreciated as we read on.

CHAPTER VII

THE ARRIVAL

THE traveller, having made the journey, is generally met on arrival by relatives or friends. The actual passage has been peaceful and without effort, like going to sleep in one place and awakening in another. All that had been treasured on earth has been left behind to become a memory.

Momentarily, he is naked in a new world, his etheric body, resembling his earth body, being the only visible thing he can call his own. He feels himself naked, and thinks of clothes—which at once appear on him. There the idea is creative, and consequently clothing appears around this naked substance, and, when friends come to greet him, his self-respect has returned. He is no longer ashamed of his nakedness.

This is how one who has had this experience put it to us:

"There are so many things on this side of life which you cannot understand yet. Of course you cannot, because I could not understand them myself when I first came over. It is a gradual unfoldment. While in earth life I used to wonder what kind of life this would be, and what clothes I would have, on the spirit side of life. In fact, I used to wonder if there was a spirit side at all; I hoped for it but was not at all certain. The day I passed out of the body I felt very much alone. I knew I was out of the body and I felt afraid. I looked down at myself and found I was nude, and then a voice out of the haze said to me: 'Come hither, my brother, and be not afraid.' I approached the light, and immediately I drew near to the light I was instantly clothed."

Thought in Etheria is a much greater reality than it appears to be on earth. Objects there, existing in tenuous etheric substance, are as real to Etherians as objects are to us on earth, but creation can come about by thought in what might be called thought substance. On earth we first image our creation and then develop it by our hands, when it becomes real to us and to other thinking creatures, but there imagination seems able to create or mould this tenuous substance without the need of hands.

So they fashion their clothes, their homes, and the subjects most dear to them by their thoughts, which thus become real to them and to others. By collective willing they can create what they wish and dispel what they wish. As they think, they are, and it is because of that they lay such stress on our mental development on earth. This difference between the two worlds is difficult to grasp, and it is one of the many surprises we shall experience when we arrive in the other world.

Surprise seems to be the predominant feeling of new arrivals. This is what we were told about their first emotional condition:

"The most surprising thing to many is to find that they are just the same and that they are not in Heaven and they are not in Hell. They are just where the good God has meant them to be for the time being. It is a beautiful world. Those they have left behind are their chief anxiety, and their greatest desire is to get into contact with them and let them know that they are still alive. That desire will be granted in time when they get a little rest and have recovered from their crossing."

Christian doctrine has misled people with regard to Heaven and Hell, and the parable of the rich man and Lazarus is no doubt largely responsible for the dogma that Heaven and Hell are separate places, and that there is a great gulf fixed between the two which neither side can cross. This, we are now told from the other side, is quite untrue. Heaven shades off into Hell and Hell shades off into Heaven by numberless imperceptible gradations. Each plane is in advance of the plane inferior to it, and consequently, from the lower to the higher planes, there is a graded system of progress. Every step forward implies an added capacity, and an increased power of enjoyment of the beautiful scenery and the perfect climate.

We were often told about the friends who will be waiting to meet us when our turn comes to make the change called death. This is what one had to say:

"They are all waiting at the Golden Gate, and when the sun shines bright on it earth will fade. I use the name 'Golden Gate' as an expression, symbolical of the entrance from the physical to the spirit side of life where you shall all meet again and there is no parting. Here all misunderstandings are cleared away, and the little pin-pricks prick no more, and every tangled thread is straightened out for ever. Here we are all brothers and sisters, helping and cheering each other on our eternal journey through life."

A relation in Etheria of a lady present once said:

"You will get many beautiful surprises when you come over here, and one of these will be when you meet your Mother. She was the finest little lady that I ever knew in earth life."

A Scotsman put it this way:

"I am no' deid (dead), ye ken—there are nane (none) of us deid. We have just reached the land of light supernal that gleams so bright afar. We have reached our home eternal. We have met our loved ones there."

Help, guidance, and friendly advice are always available for the new arrival. This is what was said during the Second World War, when so many were passing over at an early age:

"No one is left alone on coming over here; not one passes the border-line without some ministering one receiving them, and they are the more favoured who get their own friends. Many of those who are coming over at the present time are not conscious of their passing. They have given little, if any, thought to the spiritual side of life while on the Earth Plane, and they are very confused. They had not been schooled in the way of life that you, my friends, have been. You know what to expect in a general way, but they had not that knowledge."

Another time, we received this graphic description of what the passing over meant to one who had hope, but lacked knowledge:

"It is only a voice from the other shore towards which you are all travelling, but you are more fortunate than some of us. We made the journey in the bygone days without your knowledge and understanding. Nearly all of you have some understanding of life on this side. I do not mean those present, but people in general do know more positively that there is something beyond the terminus. To me it was a problem. I did not disbelieve it, but I could not fully grasp it. Oh joy of joys, when the time came when I reached the end of the road! I had no doubts, no dubiety, about the other side of life then. That shining light which greeted me as I left the old tenement of clay dispelled all doubts, and that lovely face which I had loved so long, long ago, was the first to smile on me. I saw the light from the other shore while in the body. I was hoping for it, but I had no certainty. I was hoping and dared to think that my hopes would be realised, and, oh joy of joys, just the one I wanted most was the one dear face that through the mists looked down on me."

Another put it this way:

"There are many bright forms on the other side of life waiting to greet you when you come over, all loving you as I love those I left behind in earth life. You could not but love when you have such a one as I have to love."

Those who are sad and weary on earth can get this comfort:

"There is not a weary soul on our side of life. If there are weary ones when they first come over, there are always those who help them and show them the way."

So that we shall be able to recognise our friends who have gone before, when our time comes to greet them once again, they make themselves appear as we knew them on earth:

"Those who love you on your side of life, and come here before you, will cling around your plane and will try to pick you up just as they left you in the old days, and then you will all progress together. There is nothing lost. It is only a case of 'gone before' for a little while. There is nothing forgotten. There is no good deed, no little kindness shown, no little good thought deep in your heart, but is accounted for, and goes to perfect and beautify that emancipated soul of yours when it passes out of the physical into the spiritual side of life."

Always the stress was on conduct and character. As we sow, so shall we reap; as we are here, so shall we be there.

"It is up to yourselves, every one of you, to have a beautiful dwelling on the spirit side of life, a beautiful home. You are laying the foundations of it while you travel on earth, each one of you. Keep the shining clear light of the Father before you as you travel the devious paths of the earth life, until, in His good time, He says, 'Come hither; and take up your new duties on the spirit side of life.' Then you will find the embellishments of your labour portrayed in the dwelling which is prepared for you. God bless you and help you to make a beautiful home."

Each of us will occupy the place for which we are fitted, because the mind of each of us determines exactly our destination.

"You have a body just as you have now. Love is the 'propelling force'. The one you love best will draw you like a magnet when you come over here. She is preparing a home for you just now. Where you land depends on the life you have lived in the body. Do not get elated about yourselves, or direct your thoughts on what you can do for yourselves, but trust in the great Father God to guide you rightly.

"It has been said: 'In my Father's house there are many mansions.' These are 'states', not what many think the word implies, and you cannot acquire these states until you attune yourself even on the side of life where you are now, and after you come over, for, remember, there is progress even in the earth life."

A man, well-known in Glasgow business circles before he passed on, came often to speak to his wife, who was a regular sitter. This is what he once told us:

"Out of the turmoil of life I have reached that land which I, in a hazy way, knew existed. I believed in it, but in a hazy way. I did not realise the reality of it just so exactly as my beloved partner did, and as she would have liked me to do. I had not the clear knowledge that she had, but I know now that it is the right thing. I have met those I loved so well. There is something intrinsically right and superbly precious in doing one's duty in earth life. You understand what I mean. Every little faithful duty performed which has been on one's conscience, or one's mind, will be taken account of. I recognise, through passing, how much I missed which you dear people have from time to time been imbued with, the knowledge of the contact with the spirit side of life."

Someone in the circle once asked an Etherian on which plane he would find himself, to receive this straight answer:

"Well, that depends on the life you have lived on earth. You will go just to the plane that is most suited to the environment of the life you have lived. You understand, I hope, what I mean.

"It depends first on the life you have lived on earth, and the attitude of the mind on your spirit body when it comes to the other side of life, in what condition you will arrive. That entirely lies with yourself, with the persons themselves—you know what I mean. It depends on the life you have lived in the body, and what you have done to help others and to serve the Great Master's cause, without any thought of yourself but for the great glory of God and for the extension of His Kingdom."

From the foregoing, we notice the effect of the mind on the etheric body. The mind determines the vibrations of the etheric body, and the vibrations determine the plane on which we shall live.

On another occasion we were told:

"Your reception, and the place occupied immediately when you come to this side of life, will be in accordance with the condition you have built up on earth. There is no limit to your expansion afterwards, but I love to be near the Earth Plane as I feel I can help those who are coming over. I let my supplications arise to the Great Ruler of all the worlds—Who made them all—that this old earth which I used to inhabit will soon find peace. Let us link our prayers together; a chain of prayer is a good thing, a powerful thing, if you have faith to believe it. I will say good day now. You all look couthy (kind) and canty (cheerful) and nice. God bless you."

All who lead a decent unselfish good life on earth, and think of others as well as of themselves, will find that all is well with them when they make the change. Religious faith is a help and comfort to many on earth, but no one should rely on creedal beliefs for a place in the hereafter. This will be determined by our life, by our thoughts, our aspirations, and by our deeds. So we were told:

"When you leave the body you will find, if your life has not been a one-sided service for yourself alone, but of service to God as well as man, not by lip service but by a conscientious striving to help others, all will be well with you when you make the crossing. These are the things that count."

During the Second World War, much was said of the many lives which were being sacrificed on earth, and of their arrival in a new world. Once we heard this:

"You have no conception of the host of spirits coming to the other side of life at the present time, and it is such a big undertaking to try and help them all."

Meeting them and helping them kept them so occupied, that from time to time they gave that as a reason for their absence from previous séances. When once asked about a friend on the other side, the sitters were told by an Etherian, the mother of a lady present, that:

"I do not see him just now. We are all so busy. Now, Mr. Hart, you are the mathematician. You will know how many thousands and thousands of dear boys are coming over, and it is difficult to get in touch with the right one. We do try to help them all we can. We are all travelling home. I am speaking to you all. The people who ordinarily come to you, at Mrs. Lang's home, cannot readily come at present. They are busy otherwise. I do not forget things now, Crissie. I am sure I must have been a tremendous annoyance to you, dear, but I have got my memory now."

At times they found conditions difficult during the war:

"We are all, every one of us on this side, delighted to come, but it is a difficult matter to get through under present conditions. If we cannot speak to you properly at the present time, we shall try and return at some other time."

What follows will be a comfort to those who lost relations and friends during the war.

"May it comfort you to know that, although there are thousands upon thousands coming over at the present time, there are multitudes of ministering spirits working to help them into the pathway of peace. Give out your thoughts and your love, and we will do all we can to help."

The change from one kind of life to another was so sudden for so many, that most of these war casualties were confused and found it difficult to realise what had happened. Addressing a gentleman present, he was told by a speaker from the other side:

"Mr. Cameron, I think sometimes if you could just get a look beyond the veil at this present time, and see the chaos between the two worlds, it would make you think, and the one great urge of all these boys who are being thrown over here at the present time is to find someone, some way, of telling their friends that they are not dead. It is a very real world, friends, a very real world, and not what I had been led to expect, a heaven where there was only singing and praying. It is a lively world at the present time, and I am working hard in it."

One sitter could not understand why the speaker used the word "chaos" with reference to the other world, and said so. It is not the other world that is in chaos, was the reply, but the minds of so many new arrivals. These were his words:

"I am speaking about the chaos and the confusion of the thousands of souls who are coming over to the spirit side of life, thrown over before their time. You see what I mean. It is so unnatural to us, and to me personally. I feel it is a tragedy this killing, killing, ushering into the eternal shore of life thousands of people who are not fitted for the journey, and it is left to humble servants, such as I am, to try and point the way. There is one beautiful point about this just now, if there could be one beautiful point about it, and that is, the thought that they speedily realise that they are no longer in the body, and that they are over on this side."

This grief at earth life being cut short for so many was expressed thus on another occasion:

"What saddens us here so much is to see the young, the noble, and the good, ushered into this side of life just when they would have been of so much help to humanity. You know what I mean. They will, however, still react and affect you from this side when they come here. I am going now, good day."

Again, we were told:

"It is such a tragedy. It is beyond all words, and it is not the Will of the Great Father. It is man's thoughts and inhumanity that has brought this about. It is not the wish of the Great Ones on my side of life, but it is the confused thoughts which are in the hearts of the people in the world to-day, which has brought about this tragedy. If they had known this Truth, those who have brought about this catastrophe would never have done so. God bless you, friends."

Another time, somone present said to an Etherian on the other side that war is caused by lust for power and lust for gain, and brought about by lack of understanding.

"That is the real cause—lack of understanding. There are many in your world today who have feet of clay, but they too some day will understand. God's love overcomes all."

Ignorant of how to live righteously on earth, and ignorant of what is coming to them when they die, mankind has wasted his substance on war and superstition. So the majority arrive on the other side mystified, until they are made to understand the truth, and what has really happened to them. When one of us said he supposed many of the new arrivals will not know where they are, the reply was given:

"That is the thing, to get them to understand, for some are coming over with such confused ideas about the other side of life that it is difficult to help them."

A child in the other world once remarked:

"You would be surprised if you knew what an army of little ones are helping in this work, for they are coming over to our beautiful land without the knowledge of anything at all of what is coming to them. They see us happy and they want to join in and be happy too."

We were told that no one need be anxious about those who had sacrificed their lives during the war.

"You need not worry about those who are passing over. There is not a battle area on the whole of your plane, either on land or sea, that has not thousands of Ministering Angels to help those who suffer. Even those who are very badly mangled feel no pain. Very gently they are carried over to the other side by those who are engaged in this merciful work. They will not be allowed to suffer or sorrow. It is those who are left behind to mourn for them we are sorry for, more particularly for those who have not the bright hope and knowledge which you have here, who know that dear ones gone are out of all care and trouble, their struggles over, and they are home at last among friends."

This was told us at another séance:

"It is nice to know, after life's turmoil and trouble, we can reach this haven of rest, this home of peace, and can still do what we will to help one another along life's path. I am looking after some of the dear boys who are coming over at present, who have mothers in the earth life who are sad about them, wondering how it can be God's will that they should be taken. We try to impress upon them that their boys can still be very close to them, but my duty does not stop there.

"I meet those boys and try to comfort them with the knowledge that they have now done with the earth life and have entered into a new and fuller life."

Another said:

"It is very difficult to tune in to your conditions just now. The vibrations around you are so difficult to manage, and more energy is taken from our reserves to try and ease the pathway, to show the light, to open the way to those who are making the crossing through this War, and that is a beautiful duty—to feel that we can bring comfort to someone, to convince them that they are no longer the tenants of their earth body."

Then once a few words of sympathy were expressed:

"God bless you all, and may the Great Master of all have pity on the old world to-day, and the sad hearts on it, on the suffering and all who suffer with them, and may this strife be speedily brought to an end. Amen. Amen."

Now, one last quotation on the subject of those who have passed over because of war and its effects:

"We are doing the best we can for you. It is not easy to direct the course of things in the world to-day, either from our side or your side. It is difficult to come into contact with those who are passing, and then go and try to console those who have lost their dear ones for a little time, for not all have the beautiful knowledge, and the beautiful understanding, that you have here, that in the body we have no abiding city and will all pass over in God's good time to The Great Reality.

"There is just such a mass of humanity coming into the spirit side of life at the present time that it is beyond the comprehension of your minds to understand it, and we cannot put it into words, but I might put it in this way: 'It is difficult to get them sorted out.' I think you will understand what I mean. Some are willing to listen and some are just as obstinate and unwilling to be led into the way that leads upwards and onwards. I say it remains possible for you in the earth life, who understand, to throw out your sympathy and your love to those who have passed over through this war, and to let your kind thoughts go out to them as comrades and friends because it is wonderful how quickly on this side of life they come to see what a foolish, foolish thing they had done to be killing and hating each other, and the feeling of enmity is soon forgotten.

"Your loving thoughts and prayers can help them to arrive more quickly at this conclusion. If you could just realise the condition of chaos in which they come over you would send all the love possible, but they are immediately put into the hands of those best fitted to help them. Every loving thought that we give helps them, and every loving thought coming from those on the earth side of life is immediately directed to those who most require it."

Some general remarks will now be given. This is what was said by friends in Etheria to their friends on earth who were present at these little gatherings. During a conversation, the grandfather of a lady present remarked:

"You will be surprised at the number of people you will meet when you come over beside us, people that have practically passed out of your recollection."

On another occasion, the son in Etheria of one of the sitters remarked to all present:

"When you come over here there is a great joy

and satisfaction in meeting with friends whom you have known in the stony path of life, who have stumbled perhaps and gone a little under, but who have always pulled up again and tried to march steadily onwards until the old tenement of clay is left behind, and the spirit, the real man and real woman, emerges to live a nobler, higher and more perfect life."

Another expressed the hope that:

"Some day the veil will be drawn aside, and I hope it will be drawn aside in a beautiful way, that will usher each of you into the spirit land beside those you love. May the Peace, the Joy, which cometh from the great 'I Am', be in your hearts and minds and your souls to-day, and guard your steps all through your journey in life, preparing the way to your beautiful home, and making those on this side rejoice in your efforts and successes, and give you a joyous entry into your life on this side."

When an elderly sitter remarked that he had not much to live for, a man in Etheria encouraged him with these words:

"The world is just beginning for you, my dear old friend. A beautiful world is just beginning. Though your friends are lost to sight, they are just starting afresh in a new and glorious experience of life. You will all have that experience by and by. Don't worry, don't faint by the way. Take up all the little crosses you meet on your journey. Shoulder them nobly. They are the stepping-stones to the brighter day and the brighter world beyond, when, duty achieved, labour done, you come home at last. God bless you."

Another Etherian had his regrets on reaching the new life. He expressed them to his wife, who was present, in these words:

"I wish I had understood this better when I was amongst you. I realise now that I missed a lot. Had I taken the opportunity of mixing with these nice friends of yours when I was in earth life, I would have understood more when I came over to this side."

A frequent speaker sent this message to his fiancée. It was passed on to her:

"Tell Mary, in a note, someone will transcribe it for you and send it on, tell her that I am waiting at the Golden Gateway until the day dawns in God's good time when her little pilgrimage is finished. I will be there with outstretched hands to meet my Mary. God bless you, Mary, from John Hardman."

Mr. Sloan, the medium, then asked someone in the circle how long it was since Mr. Hardman had died, to be answered at once by Hardman himself:

"Not dead, John Sloan, but alive, and I was very much in the land of wonder for some time. I will explain it to you, and I hope you will forgive me for taking up so much of your time. You see, I did not believe in the after-life, and when I came here I was bewildered with the wonder of the knowledge that it was all true. I did not deserve the kindness showered upon me by those who came to help me. I knew then that I had made a mistake. It is all over now, and I will try to help you, all of you who come here, if the opportunity comes, now and again. I know what it is to be lonely. That is how I felt when

I first came over, until some friends took me in hand and led me kindly along. Thank you for your kindness and consideration in listening to me. I will not interrupt you further now. When I say 'God bless you', it is not a lip service. I mean it."

On another occasion Hardman spoke as follows:

"It is a long cry from this side to your side, but I call to you now, and thank you, many of you in the lovely surroundings of this home, for the comfort you have given to me since coming to this side of life. I was one of the despondent souls of earth life who had a very poor outlook for the end of life. I went out in darkness and fear, but I was brought to the light of this side of life through the instrumentality of the friends I met in your surroundings (The Etherians who came to the séances.)

"I like the auras which I see surrounding you because I know from the colours that there is not one present who would not help where it is needed, and I say to you there is never a word or a loving thought that goes out to one on our side but it is borne immediately to the soul for whom it is intended if sent out in the right way. You may think they do not hear, but they get it immediately.

I did not believe there was life, conscious life, after physical death, but I have found a home eternal, and now I am awaiting the Great Master's time to move forward in His service. I pray to be allowed to help all those whom I left in the body who do not know this truth, so that they may not tread the path that I trod, but that their steps may be led into the path that will show them the way, as you in this little Meeting understand it. Then they will pass out to this side of life with confidence and with joy, and not in fear. I am John Hardman."

Then another time Hardman said:

"God bless you all, and for every little word and thought which you sent out to me during my stubborn time after passing, which I know many of you sent me who knew me at that time, I say thank you. They will be an embellishment in the homes which the Great Father has prepared for you on the spirit side of life, and for the love and help which you have given to my Mary I thank you all."

Everyone arrives in the other world after death, both believers and unbelievers. However, the more one knows about it the less strange and surprised one feels on arrival. During a conversation, this was said by a departed friend of one of those present:

"For the lucid way in which you portray my thoughts, I thank you very, very much, and for kindly bearing with me, one and all, a stumbling disbeliever. Oh, what will I call myself I do not really know. I do not know how to put it, but I did not believe in an after-life. I did not believe it, but could not get away from the thought that there might be something. I very speedily found out that there was something, and something far more real than I ever experienced in my earth life."

Another once told us much the same:

"I had not thought much about the next world at all in the earth life. I hardly thought about the after-life at all."

Ignorance is no sin, and when the new world breaks upon the newcomer this is what happens. A friend who was speaking from the other side was asked to make clearer something he had already said:

"I am speaking of those I meet from day to day, when they find that what they called 'death' is only the gateway into the real life, that the passing from the body means the entrance into a fuller life, with the hope and the assurance of a gradual uplifting to a nobler life and a nobler station. Even the little bit they know is just like a lever trying to lift a large stone. It lets them get a start, easing the burden, so that they can get volition to mount higher. Now that they have passed the barrier, they realise quickly that they have got into a fuller, nobler, and higher life, and that they have the chance of progress with nothing further to fear."

One of the Indians (we call them Red Indians on earth, though they are no longer coloured red in the other world) who helped the speakers to materialise their vocal organs once said:

"When you are gathered home to the spirit side of life, we will have a reunion. I mean all those we have been intimate with. We are prepared to wait, and all those who have communed with us in bygone times, and helped the Indian chiefs, as you called us then, to find our pathway into the inner circle of spirit life, we shall repay you for your labours, and give you a royal welcome to the spirit side of life when we all meet again."

Then on another occasion came the voice of a highly cultured Indian, who was a regular attender at our séances to help our friends on the other side to speak:

"God bless you all, and may you, when the journey is ended, and the evening shadows fall around you, as they fell on Greentree in his earth life too, find the beautiful surroundings of the Spirit World to be just as entrancing to you as they were to the Indian Chief when he passed over. This is Greentree speaking."

Once we were given this encouragement and helpful advice at the conclusion of a talk on poetry:

"Just wait until you come to my side, and you will understand what poetry really means. You have no conception of the loveliness of the country wherein we dwell. Take the rough places with the smooth, Ladies and Gentlemen, and do your little bit while you are in the body. Serve God and help your fellow men and sister women, and all will be well with you when the parting comes. Just think of the friends you have known in bygone days, the loved ones, the specially beloved ones who will be waiting to say to you 'my darling, come home'."

Those of us advanced in years will find help and comfort from the following, spoken by one who was a regular communicator. It was in reply to a sitter who had referred to the disabilities of old age:

"I came to the same time on my earth travel myself, and you are all coming to the time when you will find the difficulties of life coming very near to you, even in walking, and in speaking—conveying your thoughts in the concise way that you would like to do. You seem to lose these gifts for a little time, but they are all returned again on this side of life."

Absence from one another in time causes love to become less intense, but it does not die, and will revive when we meet again.

"I am afraid that 'All in harmony' is a phase which cannot be acquired completely on your side of life. Here we have complete harmony which knows no barrier; that love which never dies. That is one thing God brings into your heart in the earth life, and, if it is true love, it will never die. It may dwindle a little, or twinkle like a star, but at the end of the road, when you meet again, it will be illuminated once more and bright, when the trammels of clay have been thrown off, and you are received bright and beautiful into this glorious land."

Once as a séance was about to close, we heard the following:

"We hope we have been able to bring you a little further knowledge of life on our side and a little blessing to yourselves as well. We are not in a position to do unto you all that we would wish, but we are in a position to open up the path a little ahead of you. Our wish is that in every day of your earth life you may progress in the knowledge of truth—the knowledge that beyond these passing scenes there is the Eternal Reality. Because, as you all know, you will come to the passing, the demarcation line, when you will say good-bye to earthly things and pass to the more beautiful, lasting, and abiding things of the world which lie beyond, where all you love and are dreaming of will be there at the end of the road.

"I often think of that which is supposed to be a comedian's song; it is one of the most beautiful expressions I have heard. Of course, it was not the friend who sings the song who made it. It was composed for him, and the meaning behind it expresses a beautiful thought. The road may be rough and hard and stony, but at the end—all those you have loved, and who love you will be 'there at the end of the road'. I will be there. I will be there."

Another time came the name and the voice of a lady, the wife of the medium, a much loved friend of some of the sitters, who had passed on some years previously:

"God bless you, Mrs. Lang, I just want to come and speak to you myself. It is Nanna (Mrs. Sloan). I am remembering the many happy times we used to have in the old days. You are climbing the hill now, Mrs. Lang, and in God's good time, I do not want you to come too soon, but I will be there to meet you with all the others, and we will rejoice, and your dear husband and your dear son will be there also. It is just wonderful to have all your dear ones around you. I have many of mine over beside me, and, of course, I still have my dear old grumbling man on your side, but he does not mean it."

Once, when her "dear old grumbling man" expressed the desire to be free for ever of earth trials and sorrows and be with her, she replied:

"Yes, I know that, dear. I think most people when they reach your time of life and those they love have gone before them, are anxious to get away, but you must wait God's good time, dear, and then we will meet and be the same to each other as we were in the earth life."

Finally, here are three short remarks applicable to this chapter:

"It is up to each one of you stalwarts to scatter the seed of truth, and see that it falls on good ground.

Let the world know that there is no death in God's great garden of love."

A lady in Etheria, a friend of one of the sitters, after giving her name sent messages to all her family, naming each one correctly, to end by saying:

"The time will come when we will all meet again in this land so bright and free from pain."

Once, when a séance came to a close, the medium's son in Etheria said the last words, and they are a fitting ending to this chapter, which comprises what we were told we may expect when we arrive at the further shore.

"This is Dougal Sloan speaking to you. Good night, Dad. Cheerio, everyone. I will come again, and I will meet you on this side again. Be bright, be happy, and be joyful."

In the next chapter we are told about the world the new arrival has reached, and what it feels like to be there.

CHAPTER VIII

THE OTHER WORLD

ANOTHER world surrounds and interpenetrates this world on which we live. It is real to those who live there, but unreal to us on earth. It is invisible to us, but visible and tangible to its inhabitants. Some day we shall live there and, this being so, anything we can learn about it is of vital interest to everyone. Nevertheless, most people go through life with little or no appreciation of the fact that an invisible but very real world surrounds us.

To understand how another world can exist and yet not be seen and felt by us, is only possible by those who have some knowledge of physics, the science comprising the sensed and unsensed vibrations which make up the universe. Our sight, our hearing, our touch, our sense of smell, in fact our entire consciousness of existence is the result of vibrations, because physical matter and the entire physical universe is made up of vibrations which affect our senses and make us conscious of life.

We sense these vibrations, and thus they are real to us, but there are other vibrations we do not sense. Consequently, they are unreal to us, but, when we die and use as our vehicle of sense and expression the etheric body, which on earth interpenetrates our physical body, what is now real will become unreal, and the unreal will become the real. The invisible will become the visible and the visible become the invisible.

This matter of vibrations is fully considered in my book *On the Edge of the Etheric*, and the two books which followed it, namely, *The Rock of Truth* and *The Unfolding Universe*, but here we are concerned with what Etherians have to tell us from their invisible world of greater vibrational frequency.

When I became convinced that the voices speaking to me at Sloan's séances were those of living men and women, inhabiting a different order of nature from the one to which we are accustomed, I set about to find out all I could about this new world. Here I now give the information I have obtained at different times over a space of thirty-five years about the make-up of this invisible world.

On one occasion, when I was sitting alone with the medium, except for my secretary who took down in shorthand everything said on both sides of the veil at that little meeting, I put a question. I sat with my ear close to the medium's mouth, his hands held in mine, and the answer came in a man's cultured voice, clear and distinct, from the void and not from the medium. I was sure of that. This was the question I asked: "What is contained in what we call space?" and this was what I heard:

"Interpenetrating your world is another world of substance in a higher state of vibration to the one you sense. The universe is one stupendous whole, but you only appreciate what you see and hear and feel. Believe me, there are other worlds of substance, finer than physical matter, in which life exists and of which you on earth can form no conception. Connected with your earth is this world to which I came after what you call death. Encircling your world are planes of different density, and these move in rotation with the rotation of the earth."

Then I asked if his world was a material world like ours, or a dreamlike mental world, to which he replied:

"Our world is not material, but it is real for all that, it is tangible, composed of substance in a much higher state of vibration than the matter which makes up your world. Our minds can, therefore, play upon it in a different way than yours can on the material of your world. As our mind is, so is our state. To the good their surroundings are beautiful, to the bad the reverse."

Later that same evening the same voice confirmed the foregoing in these words:

"We do not live in a dream world. As I have said, we live in a real tangible world, though the atoms composing it differ from the atoms which make up your world. Our minds can act on this tangible substance in a way yours cannot do on your world. You live in a world of slower vibrations."

"So you do not live in a world of your own," I said, to which my informant replied:

"Everyone lives in a world of his or her own, you do and so do I, but if you mean can each of us see and feel the same things, I answer, Yes. All in the same plane can sense the same things. We have the same world as you have, but in a finer state."

"And you have all the sensations we have on earth?" I asked.

"Yes, we can touch and feel, and enjoy all the sensations you do."

Then came a long and more detailed statement which reveals how real life is to the inhabitants of

Etheria. In clear and measured words my informant gave me a graphic picture in words of life in his world. This is what he said:

"All in the same plane can see and touch the same things. If we look at a field, it is a field to all who look at it. Everything is the same to those in the same condition of mental development. It is not a dream. Everything is real to us. We can sit down together and enjoy each other's company just as you can on earth. We have books and we can read them. We have the same feelings as you have. We can have a long walk in the country, and meet a friend whom we have not seen for a long time. We all smell the same aroma of the flowers and the fields as you do. We gather the flowers as you do. All is tangible, but in a higher degree of beauty than anything on earth. Here we have no decay in flower or field as you have. Vegetable life just stops growing and disappears. It dematerialises.

"There is a similarity here to what you call death. We call it transition. In time, as we develop sufficiently, we pass on to another plane from which it is not so easy to come back to earth. This we call the second death. Those who have passed through the second death can come back and visit us in our plane, but we cannot go to them until we have passed through it also. This is what your Bible calls the second death. Those who have passed through it do not often come and speak to you on earth directly by materialising, as I am doing now; but they can pass their messages on to me, or someone in my plane, and we pass them on to you."

Etheria is similar to this earth, but of different substance. So when I asked what would happen to their world if our earth were destroyed, the answer came:

"It would make no difference if your earth came into collision with another star or planet and was destroyed. Our world is quite independent of physical matter."

When we come to realise that the universe is made up of vibrations of intense and rapid frequencies, of what we postulate as the ether of space, the foregoing is not so difficult to comprehend. All we see and sense is the physical universe at frequencies of 34,000 to 64,000 waves to the inch, or 400 billion to 750 billion waves a second. These produce the colours which make up the rainbow. That is between the infra red and the ultra violet, which make up the visible spectrum. (See chart at end of book.) Beyond this there are frequencies we do not sense which are worlds in themselves, or rather, they make up different worlds called spheres, the surfaces of which are called planes. Mental development controls the frequencies which constitute the etheric bodies of the Etherians. Consequently, as they think, they are. As they are, so is the plane they inhabit, as its frequencies correspond to the frequencies of the etheric body.

So we shall now read what was said at other séances on this important subject of vibrations:

"Our substance, like yours, is just vibration and so is our light. Our substance consists of what is equivalent to your electrons and protons. It is only a question of degree between us. Our substance is vibrating faster than is yours. Each surface reflects the vibrations from the etheric sun with which it is in harmony. Our progress from lower to higher planes is simply an experience of the world opening, as the result of our enlarging minds."

When asked about the difference between our world and their world, I was told that with them:

"The vibrations are faster and finer. This applies to each plane; that is, the higher, the faster and finer the vibrations."

And when they wish to come back to the slower vibrational frequencies of earth, I was told:

"Trees, houses, hills and vales exist on every plane from the physical plane upwards. When we have lowered our vibrations down to the physical plane we experience what exists on your earth's surface. The flowers and trees are brighter on our hills than they are in the vales; it is a matter of light."

Thus they can leave their surroundings, which are similar to ours, come through their surface, or lose touch with their normal etheric vibrations and appreciate physical vibrations. In this way they keep in touch with what goes on on earth. This is what I was told:

"We lower our vibrations and pass through our surface. We then adjust our vibrations to those of your earth. It is easier to get through some places than others, as they have been regularly used, and can be called throughways or highways from our plane to your earth."

These visitations can be better understood when it is realised that:

"The first plane is quite close to the earth. There is a distance between each plane, but distance does not mean quite the same thing on this side as it does to you on earth."

Moreover, these spheres, of which the planes are the surfaces, move round with the earth and, like our atmosphere, are always in the same place. This means that our friends and their surroundings always remain above us. Unless they travel to other parts of their world, as we do, to China or Australia for instance, they inhabit a country above, in space, the one they inhabited on earth. So we are not far wrong if we imagine a large invisible British community in Etheria, which once inhabited Britain, settled above us in space, and the same with the other countries of this earth. The inhabitants for some time remain settled above the country in which they once lived when on earth and, so long as the memory lasts, they continue to take an interest in it and its inhabitants. This is what was said:

"These planes move with the earth and form part of its orbit. The first plane is a kind of Clearing Station where the different nations live together. Family Life is most important, and the members await relatives of their generation to go on together to the next plane. So far as the first plane is concerned it does exist above the surface of the earth, but it is also in connection with the earth plane."

When I asked once if we could think of the first plane as like the surface of the ocean, and the earth surface as the bed of the sea, the imaginary water being the substance through which they can travel back to earth, and we, when we die, reach them, I was told:

"It is true that the etheric planes are above and

around the earth, but the first plane is close to the earth. The reference to the bed of the ocean can only be accepted as a simile. We have nothing quite corresponding to your earth vision of the ocean bed, which we can give as an illustration of what your surface looks like when you are coming to us from earth."

How do they see their surroundings? Without light nothing can be seen. They tell us that they have no night, and constant reference is made to their light. Whence then does it come? That problem intrigued me, and I asked them many questions on this subject. Here are the answers:

"Yes, we are living just above you and can come to you instantly. We have very bright diffused light which is very much more pleasant than the light from your sun, as it is not so glaring."

Another put it like this:

"Our atmosphere is naturally luminous, and extends much higher than does your atmosphere. On the first three planes there are shadows, but beyond these they get less and less definite as the atmosphere becomes more luminous. Just as there are shadows so there is shade."

And at another time I was told:

"We have no night here as you understand night."

Once at the close of a séance we said, "Good night," and this is what we heard:

"There is no night in God's great land of love. Good day, and a bright morning for all of you after your rest."

Much the same was said on one occasion during the War:

"I will not say good night. There is no night where I am, no blackouts here."

"But if you want sleep and rest, what happens then?" I once asked, towards the close of a séance.

"If we feel we want rest we can get subdued light; not so subdued as you understand it, but sufficient to enable us to rest. We have no night here as you would understand night. We get our light from the source of all light, but I cannot continue further to-night as the power has gone, so good night, and may the Light that lightens all darkness lead you into the light you are so earnestly seeking."

To be confirmed on another occasion in these words:

"We get subdued light, but not so subdued as you experience."

"But where does your light come from?" I asked.

"We have a sun and a greater sense of its invigorating power than you have of your sun. We should feel very lifeless without it. It is present on every plane, and produces colours more varied and beautiful than are yours. Only a portion of the etheric sun's vibrations are reflected on each plane. We are conscious of those in harmony with the plane on which we live, just as you are of those which are reflected by your plane."

Another Etherian described their sun in these words:

"We receive our light emanations from our etheric sun, concentric with your sun, whence comes light of great splendour, and this is reflected to our eyes by the vibration of our substance, just as is your light by the vibration of earth substance. The reason for our not having darkness is because the rays of our sun are reflected by our atmosphere at a greater height than are the rays of your sun."

This greater luminosity of their atmosphere was confirmed in other words on another occasion:

"We have day and twilight. Our atmosphere can reflect our sun's rays for a longer time than yours can, so we have twilight instead of night. We do not need sleep as you do, so we do not miss having no night."

It seems as if the process of light reflection from their sun is much the same with them as is the process with us. The higher the atmosphere, so is the reflection greater. When those parts of the etheric planes are away from the etheric sun the luminosity of their atmosphere gives them light. We on earth experience the rays of the sun of the same frequency as are the vibrations of physical matter, and the etheric sun's rays are reflected on the various planes by vibrations of the same frequency. The sun is emitting vibrations in harmony with the earth, the first plane, the second plane, and so on. Our atmosphere does not extend so high as does their atmosphere and its reflection is not so extensive as is their reflection. Consequently we have night but they have twilight.

A much fuller explanation, with diagrams, of how we appreciate the colours produced by our sun will be found in *The Unfolding Universe*. Just as our sun sends out rays through the ether which are reflected by the vibrations of physical substance to our eyes, so they tell us that:

"Our etheric sun sends rays through the ether

and these are reflected to our eyes by substance. Consequently, like you, we experience colours but they are more brilliant and varied than are yours."

Another emphasised this in these words:

"We get our light from the source of all light, a great central force. Its brilliance depends on the distance the plane is from this source."

And this gives light which was described in these words:

"Our light is soft, radiant, brilliant, beautiful and blending."

I have been told that the luminosity of their sun prevents it being seen, but its light produces colours beyond our imagination. Consequently Etheria is a beautiful world, a fact which was emphasised repeatedly, and, as their words were always correctly recorded at the time, let us read what they told us once of the beauties of the world in which they live:

"If I could just take you by the still waters and through the green pastures, through our lovely gardens, and show you our hillsides, our mountain ranges, and all the beauties of this wonderful country. Flowers that bloom in all colours which you will never know in the earth life, and which never fade and decay. The beautiful birds that sing in the trees, without fear. It is a wonderful country, and I worship the thought of the Mighty Chief who made it all, the Happy Hunting Ground. I found, when I came to this side, dear friends, it was not a hunting ground, unless it was hunting for friends known on earth, and who were as anxiously seeking for me."

The foregoing was said by a Red Indian, but a Scotsman, who had lived and died in Glasgow, put it thus when speaking to his daughter who was present:

"I wish I could just transport your vision to the great beauties of the Summerland and show them to you all. There are no words of mine, I cannot just put it in the way I would like, that can describe the beauty and the calm majestic grandeur of the beautiful lands which we visit. Ours is a beautiful world, it is just gorgeous. The Glasgow Botanical Gardens are not to be compared with the exquisite gardens we have here."

Another native of Glasgow, now in that beautiful world, told her sister who was present:

"Oh, Jean, it is beautiful, and I have such a dear little cottage to stay in with a beautiful garden. I had never seen such a lovely garden before with glorious flowers of all colours, flowers that you never see on earth, and they do not fade. They bloom all the time, and, when you pick them, others just seem to come in their place. What beautiful perfumes they have, and, Jean, there is honeysuckle growing up at each side of my door, masses of it. I just wish you could see it, it is so lovely, but you will see it some day, dear. I will show it to you."

The husband in Etheria of a lady present once spoke these words to his wife:

"My darling, I wish I could find adequate words to describe to you the beautiful country that, in God's love and goodness, I have been allowed to land in. Across the border-line I am reunited with you and those whom I loved so well while in earth life. Be steadfast and true, keep fighting onwards, never get downhearted. There is a bright day coming."

A lady present was told this by a friend in Etheria:

"I would fain have you see the beautiful home where I dwell, far superior to anything I knew in earth life. I was in a humble position in my earth life, but the Good Father, as I was told, had prepared this place for me, which I attained to in a short time. I listened patiently to all that the big teachers had to say in the Auditorium, and I found the way, the pathway that led to my beautiful home on the spirit side of life. It is just the place I would have desired had I chosen it for myself."

When I once asked about the vegetation, I received the reply:

"Our vegetation is something similar to yours, but much more beautiful."

A schoolmaster present once heard this said in front of him during a long conversation with a friend on the other side:

"We cannot all enjoy the same appreciation of the beauties round about us. Some things appear more beautiful to one than to another, and we carry that feeling over here until we advance further in this lovely land towards perfection."

Their mental development in Etheria determines more than it does here their attitude to their surroundings. As they think, so they are, and undeveloped people are on lower planes than those more developed. To reach the higher life each mind must unfold, as this Etherian discovered:

"Well, it was a disappointment to me when I came over, because I was a long time on the spirit side of life before I realised I was actually out of the body. The surroundings were so similar to earth surroundings, and I had not been taught to expect that. Then I thought I would be with my old friends that I had liked so much, and I was not. The most remarkable thing was that there were some people whom I had not cared for much in earth life who were my best friends on this side. You know, I wanted to get beside my darling old Mother, but discovered that I had a long way to travel before I could do so. She came and spoke to me. She was the first to greet me when I came here, but I could not go with her."

One of the sitters here remarked that he thought that once we had passed over there was no separation from those we loved, to hear in reply:

"I am telling you, of course, of my earliest experiences on this side of life. I have progressed much since then and I am now often with my Mother, though I have not advanced sufficiently to be with her always. I am much with my Father also. It is a beautiful country I am now living in."

The Universe unfolds as our mind develops. As it develops we advance from plane to plane. So, when one of us once remarked that there seemed to be no limit to our progress, the friend on the other side who was speaking exclaimed:

"You have struck the key, Sir, according to what I am learning over here, there is no limit to our surroundings. Of course, I have not advanced very far as yet, and have not had much experience."

On another occasion, a departed friend of one of the sitters confessed:

"I did not understand this Truth in earth life—you know what I mean—and it now presses on my soul with a gladness and joy that is overwhelming. I am bursting to tell you about the beauties of this land which I did not believe existed."

He repeated this confession of his enlightenment when speaking to us at another séance:

"You know I went over in Doubting Street, but I landed in such a lovely, lovely home, far beyond my deserts."

Here we come to the end of what our etheric friends had to tell us about the world in which they live. There, with their minds more powerful, and yet more sensitive, than are our minds on earth, they can control and appreciate their surroundings in a way impossible for us to understand. To the good these are beautiful, to the wicked the reverse.

To be able to determine their surroundings by thought, and yet to have a mind so sensitive that our thoughts on earth can be picked up if they so desire, reveals a higher state of being than exists on earth. Here, mind is greatly subject to the body, there the body is subject to the mind. Here, mind is so in subjection to substance that thought has not the same power and influence as it has there, where to think is to be. As the mind is, so is the state of being. Nevertheless their substance, though not material, is real and tangible at a much higher frequency, or state of vibration, than is physical substance, and their minds can therefore play upon it, mould it, and use it in a way we cannot do with matter on earth.

This information we can only accept as best we can, and some day enlightenment will come for everyone. Meantime we shall proceed, and read in the next chapter what they had to tell us about the conditions in which they live.

CHAPTER IX

CONDITIONS IN THE OTHER WORLD

WE have just been reading about the nature of the other world. Now we shall learn about the conditions in which Etherians live. Their minds, as we have discovered, control their lives, and they can move easily from place to place. The good cannot live with the evil, or the evil with the good, as a mental barrier protects the good from the bad.

Etherians can mould their surroundings by thought in a way we cannot imagine, and they can be where they wish to be so easily that the conditions in which they live are in this respect greatly different from ours on earth. Nevertheless, though it is largely a mental world, yet it is not a dream world, as all on the same plane experience the same way of life. Their countryside, its climate, its scenery, its houses and vegetation are the same to all on the same plane, and its people are individuals like those we come in contact with each day on earth.

This I know, because I enquired, and this is what I was told:

"Our world is very real to us, but the conditions in which we find ourselves depend on the condition of our mind. If we wish it we can be surrounded by beautiful country. Our mind plays a large part in our life here. Just as we live in surroundings suitable to our mental development, so we also attract to ourselves minds of the same type as our own. Like attracts like in this world. So also like attracts like so far as your world and our world are concerned. The evil-minded here are attracted by the evil-minded in your world, and the good here by the good with you. We can, at will, take on earth conditions by lowering our vibrations. Our bodies become heavier and more perceptible to the human eye, which accounts for our being seen at times by those who have the faculty on earth of sensing our vibrations."

When I once asked if they live together on a surface as we do on earth I was told:

"The general answer is 'Yes'; but it must be remembered that there are earth-bound souls who do not arrive at the first plane without assistance, and in some cases for a very considerable time, so far as time is reckoned on earth. There are special places for children to be brought up in, as well as healing stations for those who come over, and other healing stations for those living on the first plane. But the word 'place' does not quite signify the same thing as is meant by it on the earth plane."

What are called the higher planes are reached by mental development, because the individual mind has fitted the etheric body to be in harmony with that more exalted form of life. The vibrations of these higher planes are more frequent than those of the lower planes, and life there is consequently more intense. So we once heard the following:

"We use our own thought vibrations to reach the higher planes. You know there are planes and planes on our side of life that I have not evolved to yet, and to which I cannot hope to attain for a long time to come, but I have had conversations with, and the company of, those who live on these planes. They are able to come to us but we cannot go to them till we evolve a little higher."

Those in harmony with a lower plane find the next higher plane too intense for comfort and cannot live there, but those in the higher planes can come back to the planes of lower vibration by mental concentration:

"We lower our vibrations by mental effort. It is easy for those on a higher plane to go to the lower, but those in the lower cannot go to those in the higher. Those coming from higher planes bring with them their atmospheric or rather their etheric vibrations."

Mental development brings about a classification of the inhabitants of the various planes which make up Etheria. Each one determines where he or she will live. The desire for mental harmony brings together those who think alike, but love is a strong force of attraction. When we were discussing the power of love on one occasion, someone asked the Etherian who was speaking if one could always be with the person loved. He replied:

"Yes, if you are in the same vibration spiritually, that is so. If not, they can be often with us, but we cannot live in their surroundings. There is what we term here a 'classification'. We are among the friends we are worthy of being with immediately. If we have lived a good and worthy life on earth, we immediately go into a condition consistent with the life we have led. We would not be happy if we were in a condition we were not attuned to. You can move to a different home in the old world, according to your tastes and position, but a different method obtains here, where we can only go to the place and condition we have attained spiritually."

This answer was confirmed on another occasion in these words:

"There is a place, an allotment, for all classes when you 'shuffle off this mortal coil'. It is up to everyone to make their own Paradise on this side by the life you live while in the body."

Though there is a place for everybody, yet those who live on different planes meet each other, as the following answer to a question makes clear:

"Certainly, I have met your father. I see him frequently, though we are not living in the same country as it were. We are on different planes."

Family life often continues, and love seems to be a stronger force there than here. Their affection for loved ones on earth is very noticeable, and the pleasure they get in speaking to friends and relations on earth can easily be observed by the tone of voice:

"We are all one family, all brothers and sisters, and we acquire the knowledge that the Great Teacher wants us to obtain. We must stay in the surroundings we find ourselves in until we acquire the knowledge necessary to pass to higher planes, and, having ability to rise, we obtain the counsels of the great leaders. There are things you cannot know, until you come to this side of life, educated as you are, as you have all become, and as we all must become in time."

Many are surprised on arrival in Etheria, as ignorance of the subject on earth is so profound that few know anything of value. Religious creeds may help the dying, but they are of no help to the new arrivals who have been taught superstition during their earth lives and not what is true. Such is evidently what this Etherian thought:

"When I came here, it was not what I expected. I thought I was going right into the Kingdom of Heaven right away, and was disappointed, but I did find I was in the Kingdom of Friends right away. I am only speaking of my own experience, remember. I was just an ordinary fellow in my earth life, and did not think much at all of the life to come, and when I did get here I expected to have all those I had loved beside me always, but that did not happen."

He, like so many, had probably relied on a saviour to secure for him a place in the Kingdom of Heaven, little realising that no scapegoat can suffer for our sins and wickedness, and that as we live on earth so shall we be hereafter. We go to the place for which we are mentally fitted, as someone on the other side once told a gentleman visitor to the circle:

"There are many from the spheres beyond who come to my plane, but I cannot go to theirs, and you will find there are many of your loved ones, who love you well, who will be on a different sphere from you, and until you rise to a condition of spirit equal to theirs you cannot be in constant contact with them, though you may have them often in your company."

A relation of one of the sitters once gave this description of Etheria in reply to a remark made by someone present:

"We often go long walks—it is a beautiful country. I wish I could explain to you the scenes beyond scenes which open to one's view. Well, Sir, the vistas and scenes on this side of life—I cannot call them anything other than different worlds—are so vast; worlds and worlds beyond worlds, and all vibrating at different rates of movement, higher and higher vibrations, but all is happiness and joy complete. Sometimes we radiate in the surroundings of those whom we have known for a long time but who have gone on, and spend a beautiful time with them—just as you would do in earth life when going to visit friends, and then we come back to our associations again."

"Do you pass through a second death to have this experience?" he was asked.

"I am speaking about visiting these places, but we always return. It is all done by radiation, by vibration, and when we go on a visit we cannot go by ourselves, we have not the power, but friends from these spheres come for us and lend, or put forth, some of their own power to enable us to attain these higher levels for a short period only. We could not stay until we have attained that degree of spirituality which would enable us to live there without discomfort. We enjoy these brief visits. They are so edifying, so beautiful, but I am always glad to get back to my own surroundings where I live amongst friends more attuned to my own condition."

During a conversation with her grandfather a lady present was told:

"Most people who come to the spirit side of life expect to be in the same surroundings all the time as the ones they loved on earth. That certainly is so in many instances. It all depends on how spiritually you are akin to each other, but often those we have loved dearly are too far advanced for us to reach them. They can be with us certainly, but cannot take us with them. We have just to wait a little until we attain the condition whereby we can travel and understand the surroundings where we are going. God bless you."

Some remarks were once passed, amongst the sitters, about our difficulties as war-time travellers, when a loud etheric voice broke in and said:

"We can get about with much less trouble over here. We, what you might say, annihilate space on this side, those who have advanced to any extent, I mean. If we are doing our duty, and doing the Master's Will, by one thought we can transport ourselves from the spirit side of life, right down into your own homes. That is chiefly by doing the will of the advanced spirits who are helping us. We can only come so far, and then they take up the thread and give us the necessary power."

The expression "the Master's Will" can be taken to mean keeping within the law, as law and order exist there as here. Natural law prevails, and, when they have learned to understand it, travel is easy. This is what the medium's wife once told her husband during a long conversation with him:

"If I could only describe to you the lovely walks we have sometimes. We never tire. To cross the beautiful lakes, we can either go in a similar thing to a boat, or just be wafted over. And the fruits and the flowers, and the beauty of the verdure of the country, the magnificent feeling of well-being that one has. I wish you could just feel it. There is no waste and no decay. The flowers just fade away. You never see them decay, and then fresh ones come in their place, not in full bloom, but starting from the root."

A lady sitter once asked her sister, who was speaking to her from the other side, if a certain relation she named was with her, to receive this reply, which also confirms what was said above:

"Not to-day, but I see her from time to time. We often go—it is difficult to tell you—I was going to say long walks in the beautiful Summerland. We both loved walking, as you know, and we do not forget, dear. When we feel that we have a hill to go up, we just think of being at the top, and that takes us right up, where we can view the beauties of the spirit land. We just start off from the point we are most suited for, and have not seen the Great Master so far, but those that have been here for a very long time tell us of the beauties and the splendours that we have still to behold."

A man who, when on earth, was a prominent Spiritualist in Glasgow and a regular sitter in the early days of the Sloan circle, returned from time to time, and once remarked about the many who were sorrowing for those they had lost through death. He concluded his remarks with these words:

"It would be a consolation to them if they knew what you know about the spirit side of life, the life of peace, of security, as I have found it. I am free to roam across the great vast spaces of the spirit land in so far as my progression permits, this beautiful and wonderful land, dropping in now and again to give you a little message of love on the earth sphere. God bless you."

The medium's wife, a regular member of the circle when on earth, once expressed her great pleasure in returning to earth and rejoining her old friends:

"I enjoy it the same as when I was on earth. I can tune in to you so well, and hear the familiar sound of your lovely voices which were so sweet to me in the old days."

Then addressing by name one of the ladies present, she remarked:

"Your dear Mother does not forget things now, you know, and I have many nice walks with her."

At the same séance, this once forgetful mother of the lady present remarked to her daughter:

"Don't think that I am faltering and feeble now, but I just take on the vibrations of how I felt before leaving the body. I will show you round my favourite places. I come for you often and take you away in your sleep, and I wish you could bring back some memory of the beauties of the country I am in.

"We have gardens everywhere, you know. Father is very, very busy. You know he is a man that would never be at rest unless he was doing something for somebody, and he is like that yet. At present he has plenty of opportunities, you know, to work for those on our side. The spirit side is teeming with those who are wandering about. I hardly know how to put it, but they are coming over so quickly through this terrible strife, and need some guidance, and Father is helping there."

The stress they put on their beautiful scenery and vegetation is worthy of notice. Etheria must be a paradise for flower lovers, and ardent gardeners on earth have much to which they can look forward. A much esteemed lady now in Etheria, still looked on as a friend by most of the sitters, once remarked:

"There is perpetual growth, and no death, just a fading, and another springs up, just a facsimile of the one before, or more beautiful sometimes, just as in the human frame. When 'you shuffle off this mortal coil' and put on immortality, it is then you will expand, and go forward to the peace, the beauties of the land, the Summerland of God."

The mother of one of the sitters once said:

"It is just myself, and it is fine to speak to you across the border-line. Your flowers are just beautiful, my dear, but they are nothing to what we have on our side. They can beat them altogether. God bless you, May dear."

A very homely remark was once made to a lady present by her great-uncle, David Johnston, about himself and the lady's mother in Etheria:

"I am as happy, as happy as you could wish me to be, and that is saying a good deal, and now, my dear, dear Crissie, I do wish you could see me and your Mother—Davie and Mrs. Colquhoun—going off for a stroll. What are you laughing at? We have far lovelier scenery than you ever see on your side of life. It is similar but far more beautiful. The colours are magnificent, and there is no decay. It just seems to fade away. You see the growth from the bottom, just as you do in earth life, and when it comes to full maturity it just vanishes."

When a sitter was speaking to a number of relations now in the other world, she asked her great-grandfather if he saw much of her father. He replied, "Certainly," but they were not living on the same plane. Each was in what might be termed a different country. Then he continued:

"I may be more advanced now, but I was further back than he was to start with. We are both in beautiful surroundings, but they are different. I have much to thank God for, especially those who helped me when I first came over, because I was not sure, friends, Ladies and Gentlemen, where I was going. It is a lovely land I am living in."

Once a lady present received this personal message from a friend in Etheria. Calling her by her correct pet name she remarked:

"I am with your mother and had such a lovely walk with her before we came here, through a very beautiful part of Paradise. Do you know what we were talking about? Your mother said to me: 'If Crissie just knew how happy I am, I am sure her heart would be glad and she would not worry about me.' "

A lady in Etheria, in the course of conversation, spoke about someone known to one of the sitters. She named him correctly, and went on:

"I was with him before I came here. He took me for a beautiful walk in my country, which he told me he had not believed existed before he came here to this side of life. When he came to our side of life he found a world which he had not known was there, and I told him all about it. So he said: 'Well, you will be my guide and take me some days for walks, and now I believe in this side of life.' "

A lady in Etheria first gave her name, and spoke to her sister who was present. After referring to the talks they had about the other world when she was on earth she continued with these words:

"Yes, but I do not think I just understood it. I think you had a better grip of it, Janie, than I had, but, when I came into reality, into the beautiful home on this side of life, then I knew it was real."

In the course of conversation, a friend on the other side concluded:

"You will do that, I know, and you will find a home so very beautiful and wonderful that my tongue cannot describe it. I was singing with you to-night when you sang that beautiful little hymn you have just sung."

A very dignified voice once spoke, claiming to be that of a man who had been a Red Indian chief on earth. He came often, and was always recognised by the tone of his cultured voice The wife of one of the sitters had passed on, and the Indian addressed him in these words:

"I know very well how you feel. I have sat in the lonely wigwam myself, and I know what it is when those you love have gone away, but it was not long before my dear one came to me."

"So you knew about survival when you lived on earth?" came the reply from the gentleman addressed:

"I always knew that I was going to the Summerland, and that some day I would meet my squaw again. I found that it was so. It is a beautiful thought, Ladies and Gentlemen, to know that you are going to pick up your dear ones on the other side of life, and, oh, I would like to tell you of the beauties of the country.

"Language fails me to describe the wonderful

glories of this beautiful land that you are coming to. God bless you, my friends. You will run and not weary. You will walk and not faint. You will drink of the crystal waters that run by the side of the way. You will eat of the fruits, more glorious even than the fruit of the grape of the world. A profusion of fruits and flowers that I could not describe to you."

A lady present enquired, "But you don't eat them, do you?"

"Of course we eat them. Not in the way you eat them here in the body, but we do enjoy them."

Which fits in with the reply I once got at another séance to the same question.

"Yes, we eat and drink, but it is not what you mean by eating and drinking. To us it is a mental condition. We enjoy it mentally, not bodily as you do."

Once, when we were discussing the houses in which they live, someone asked if the beautiful flowers they so often spoke about could be picked, and used to decorate their houses. This is what we were told:

"Oh, certainly, you can decorate your homes, your houses where you live, with anything you like, and, if you are passing some place, and have seen some particular flower, and thought 'I would like to have that flower in my garden,' when you return home you will find it there. The Spirit Overseer of the various plants and flowers will bring the same plant to grow in your garden, without you troubling about it."

"Where do you put the flowers you take into your houses?" asked a practical enquirer.

"We just put them in a vase the same as in your

own house, and you don't need to worry about breaking the vases, because you cannot break them."

"And do the flowers require water?" asked the same person.

"We have a liquid, but it is not exactly water. We have the equivalent of many material things here. It would not be a real home life, if you had not the same things as you had in earth life. You see the flowers growing up here, so very beautiful, and fading away when they come to full maturity. There is no waste or decay."

My sister-in-law once told me this about what we would call water:

"Our world is very much like yours. When I arrived first of all I saw a beautiful little waterfall and went and put my hand under the water. When I pulled my hand away it was quite dry, and I did not feel the water. When we bathe in our sea we get all the pleasure and exhilaration of bathing, but we are never wet, and come out of the water quite dry."

When I asked if they came through their own surface to come back to earth, she replied:

"We come back to earth through our own surface, but it was just a question of tuning in to the vibrations of the different surface levels. Yes, we have towns and villages and everything is very beautiful, and we never have any darkness."

That Etheria is very much like our world in appearance was confirmed on another occasion, when a friend of one of the sitters told us this about the world in which he lives:

"It is just like your own world, and I have never desired to progress any further until I get some of my own people over with me. It was a consolation to me to have some of my own people meeting me, although they did not stay with me, and I cannot go where they are, but I am quite content meantime where I am. It is a beautiful place I am in, and I am doing my little best to help the boys who are coming over, to show them the best way out of their difficulties."

A lady sitter once remarked about seventy long years when talking to her grandfather. He laughed and said:

"I am laughing at you, my dear, hearing you talk about seventy long years. It is only a span; just a wink on this side. It seems no time since you were a wee bit birkie (smart kind) of a lassie running around with your wee short skirts. I feel very happy that I have managed to get the conditions which are present here to-night."

Time is different to them than with us. So when a lady present once said it was years and years since she had spoken to the Etherian who was addressing her, he replied:

"It seems such a little space to me here. Yet it must be long to you, and some of these years were weary and sad; but there was something said to-night while I was standing near you. I listened to my dear little friend repeating these words: 'Then, ah then, you will understand.' "

A sitter, an elderly man, was once told in conversation:

"Years and years seem a long time to you, but you are coming to the time when years and years will mean just nothing."

And again the question of time in Etheria was summed up in these few words:

"Time does not count with us here."

This chapter contains what we were told about conditions in the other world, but it is only a glimpse of reality. Our language is inadequate for them to express all they could tell us. Words cannot convey to us what some day we shall only learn from experience. As a well-known publisher, and author of a famous book on Spiritualism, once confessed to his grand-daughter who was present:

"I thought I knew a lot before I came here, but I have a lot to learn yet."

So we all will have much to learn when we reach the other side, and meantime let us endorse the words of a man who once spoke to all present one night at a meeting of the Sloan circle:

"We have all much to be thankful for, very much more to be thankful for, both on the physical plane, and when you get over here. You will recognise then that all I am saying is true."

I conclude this chapter by giving a graphic description of one side of life in the other world. The Etherian who spoke was the medium's wife, and she spoke fluently and with animation. What she said, as always, was heard by everyone, but she addressed a lady present whom she had known well when on earth. The remarks had to do with the welcome the members of the circle would get when they arrived in Etheria.

"You will sit at a table on my side of life, and we will have a beautiful spread for you, one that you like best. You will find no old people here, no bent backs, dim eyes or tired faces, but a band of loved ones, full of holy love and glorious youth, welcoming you to our side of life, when God's good time comes. That is for you all, God bless you. You will understand when you come here and meet those whom you love—fathers, mothers, uncles and aunts, sisters and brothers, some of them in an advanced state of years when they left the body. You will get a passing glimpse of them as you knew them last, and then they will come to you in the buoyancy of their youth as they are now. They will come in the stature and the bloom of manhood, the beauty of womanhood."

With this hopeful prospect before us we shall now pass on to the next chapter, and learn about their way of life.

CHAPTER X

THEIR WAY OF LIFE

THE way our friends, who have passed on, live is a matter of great interest to us, especially as we ourselves will some day live in the same way when our time comes to join them. Life with them seems to proceed much as it does on earth, though they have many advantages we do not possess. As with us, social and family life take a prominent place, and those intent on acquiring knowledge have every opportunity to do so. The arts, such as painting and music, play an important part in their lives, but let us read what they themselves have to say about the way they live.

When a lady present asked her father what he was doing, she received the reply:

"I am learning a great deal over here. In fact, I am attending what one might term a University, the one where this lady's son is."

He then addressed the lady referred to, in these words:

"I attend the College at which your son lectures."

On earth her son was an outstanding scholar and, had he not been killed in the First World War, the career of a University professor was the one he might well have chosen.

"And what are you learning, Father?" asked his daughter, to which he replied:

"I am learning the Way of Life,"

a few words which embrace almost everything.

Let us, however, realise their difficulty in making us understand their life in a different order of existence from our own. To begin with, they are speaking under difficult conditions, their vocal organs being materialised and consequently used in an unnatural way.

When a sitter once said that it seemed as if he had a lot to learn, he received the apt reply:

"And you will be studying many years yet before you fully understand. You will never begin to understand properly until you come to this side yourself."

On another occasion an etheric friend of one in the circle spoke to a schoolmaster present, in these words:

"I have added much to my knowledge of the spirit side of life through the valuable teaching I have received from Arthur Lang. I often go up to hear him speaking when he is lecturing. Am I making myself plain ? I do not know how I could have understood things so well if I had not heard someone like him, and such as he, explaining matters to me when I first came over, and, goodness knows, you will all need help yourselves when you come over here, though, with the knowledge you already have, you will understand it far better than I did."

The Arthur Lang referred to is the same person, the scholar, who was mentioned at the opening of this chapter.

Then on one occasion during a conversation the following remark was made:

"Well, you know, natural law was taught me on this side of life. I did not believe or think much about an after-life while I was in earth life, but dear friends early taught me the way in which I must go in order to progress here."

Then another time a schoolmaster present was told that earth is a school house and that:

"You do what you call the curriculum, for the wider life, and, if you pass fairly well, it will be all the better for you when you come to this side of life. The peace of the Great Father be with you now and in the time to come, and may the Great Master guide your thoughts, each one of you, so that you will be glad you have pursued the path of duty and worked for the good, not of yourself only, but for one and all—your brothers and sisters on the journey."

A sitter once remarked that he would like to know what the solution of life is, to be told:

"Yes, I understand—but it is there—what you call 'Solution'. There are times when travellers on the Road of Life find a bad road, a crooked road, which makes it difficult to go ahead, but there is a Light, a shining Light, which is named 'The God of Love'—the Light of Life which never dies, but burns more brightly, so that you will see better as you come towards this side, and go to those who throw their light on you, and who love you. When you come here you will get spirit eyes which will enable you to see as well in darkness as in light. You are all quite visible to me just now."

Then again the mother in Etheria of a lady who was present remarked:

"It is a peculiar thing—the web of life; different

for each one, and still it must be woven correctly. You are all weaving the web of life for yourself. You are all weaving personality and character on earth. You are living a life that will go with you when you pass the barrier, and fit you into the condition on this side that you have prepared for yourself on earth."

An interesting conversation, which the sitters were once carrying on amongst themselves, was interrupted by a lady on the other side aptly remarking:

"An open mind is a stepping-stone in the right direction, if you continue to keep it open. It is well to keep an open mind when anything new and strange is brought before you. You get time to think it out and not reject it without undue consideration. One with an open mind can take things to avizandum (private consideration) with advantage. I think you understand my meaning."

A sitter once remarked about his desire for further knowledge of the after life, to be told by the Etherian to whom he was speaking:

"We all have desires on this side as well, you know, but I may tell you that I do not get all the desires which I have on this side fulfilled or granted. Far from it, and, I have no doubt, neither will you. I got more than I deserved, all the same. Had I got my deserts, God knows where I would have been to-day."

The same sitter on another occasion asked a friend, to whom he was speaking, if he were pleased with the work he was doing over there, to be told with fervour:

"Pleased, Mr. Cameron, is not an adequate word to express it. My work is to me a joy unspeakable, the glory of service fills me with a happiness I cannot well explain. God be with you until we meet again, and may the Great Spirit hover round and shield all of you from harm. Good night, and God bless you."

Their happiness in life was the theme of a number of Etherians, and here are a few quotations from their remarks. A husband, referring to himself, and to his wife, who was with him, remarked to a relation in the circle:

"We are still happy. It is just a continuation of the life we had on earth, carried on to the other side of life for us as well."

On another occasion a lady in Etheria told her sister who was present:

"Don't worry about us. We are so happy, so very, very happy. Of course, we miss you all and the happy times we used to have."

A husband and wife are together again and very happy. A relation, called Lillian, who was present, heard this:

"Lil, it is Gladys. If you could just all know how happy my Jim and I are. (Then speaking to us all, she said): He was my husband in earth life, and we are together here. Au revoir for a while."

Another husband and wife are likewise together again:

"We are both together, your Father and I, but not all the time. I would not wish that, as I could not just go into all the pursuits that Father likes and joins in, but I have found many friends here, people whom I did not know in earth life, but who claim kinship with me. We are all more intimate with one another on this side."

This naturally leads us on to think of their home life. Where and how do they live? They speak of their houses, their homes and their children, but the children referred to are those they had on earth. I have never heard of children being born in Etheria, but I have been told of earth children being adopted, if I may use this word, by Etherians who are fond of children. In this way the children who die on earth find homes, and some join their parents when they in turn leave this earth for the other world.

So I once asked about the houses in which they live.

"Our houses are just as we care to make them. Your earth houses first were conceived in your mind and then physical matter was put together to make them as your mind first saw them. Here we have the power to mould etheric matter as we think. So our houses are also the products of our minds. We think and we construct. It is a question of thought vibrations, and so long as we retain these vibrations we can hold the object, which during this time is objective to our senses."

That their houses are as real to them as our houses are to us is evident from the reply a mother in Etheria gave to her daughter on earth. "Have you a nice home?" her daughter asked.

"Yes, but I have not seen much of my own home recently. I have been on a round of visits—staying with different people—sometimes for such a long time that I hope I do not overstay my welcome."

"I am sure you would never do that," remarked her daughter, and this was her reply:

"I do not seem to, for they are all so glad to see

me. I have met many people here I knew long ago and had almost forgotten about, but they all knew me and are so anxious to have me with them. I have a wonderful body now, Jeanie. I am not aged now, you know, and can enjoy going about."

On one occasion, this very homely bit of news was conveyed to a lady present from her grandfather:

"I am William Johnston. It is William Johnston speaking to Crissie Colquhoun. Hello, I was just speaking to your Mother, and saying: 'Oh, if Crissie could just see us all sitting here on this beautiful day, out on this lovely lawn, how she would enjoy to mix with us.' It was just a reunion to commemorate something which your Grandfather likes to remember to-day, as you would call it to-day. Our memories go out to you just now, and Mother wants me to try and throw out my thoughts to you so that you can realise and understand what is taking place."

How natural it all is! We arrive in Etheria in a natural way, without any passport to enable us to enter, and, when we get there, we live the kind of life we lived on earth. We meet again our friends we knew on earth, and we ourselves determine exactly where and how we shall live.

Nevertheless, on this natural fact, has been built up all the world's supernatural religions, with their saviours, their priests, theologians, churches, temples, mosques, synagogues, pagodas and other holy places. A natural event has had woven round it ideas which are termed sacred or holy, and a mystic atmosphere has gathered, to produce holy books, sacred literature, sacred music, holy days, mysticism, theological colleges, convents and monasteries, besides multitudes of monks and nuns who live apart from the rest of mankind in the hope of a life nearer to God hereafter.

On this natural event, namely death, much of history has turned, religion being the cause of half the story of mankind, besides the reason for the misery, the intolerance and slaughter of untold millions of men, women and animals. Who can fathom the number of deaths, the suffering and the waste caused by religious wars, persecution and sacrifice, all of which was brought about by mankind's ignorance of what happens after death?

As we sow, we reap, as our mind is, so we live. This was once explained to us in these words:

"Yes, I am trying to explain to you how we build our home by deeds done in the body. Any little good I had done in earth life which had been a bit of a sacrifice to me, made my home, my beautiful home, more beautiful, and any kind thought I had, any kind action I did, all went to the beautification of my Paradise of Peace, my home, my garden, in all its beauty, and the flowers I love tending as I used to do in earth life. They grow from the little plants to the full fruition of all their beauty and fragrance, and then they just vanish and others grow in their place. There is no decay; no toil in gardening. I have such a wonderful home and I just came to tell you about my house and my garden."

Another once put it like this:

"You cannot think, you cannot understand—I hope I am not interrupting just now—but every little word that you broadcast in the world to-day, of your thoughts and your ideas of the spirit side of life, if you portray them to those travelling along life's journey, to those who do not know this truth, it will help them to understand when the dark days come about their pathway. They have not the knowledge that you have, and it will be another brilliant gem in the structure of the house where you are going to reside in on the spirit side of life.

"Thought is a stupendous word. Your thoughts, they reach so far, and the tentacles of these thoughts not only reach North, South, East and West, but they reach all round everywhere. Have kind thoughts, Ladies and Gentlemen, have loving thoughts, and, above all, have pure thoughts. God bless you and guide you ever on that bright road wherein walks nothing that is evil, and into the clear light, the light of love which ends in the rest of eternal day."

Again the same idea was expressed by a man in the other world, when thanking a sitter for passing on to his fiancée a message he had sent to her at a previous séance:

"Thank you for the comfort and joy you have brought to my Mary. It will be a beautiful stone, a jewel in the beautiful home that awaits you on the spirit side of life. All the beautiful thoughts which you have sent out will be an embellishment to that home. It is not so far distant when I thought such a thing would be impossible. I thought there was no after-life, but oh, I am here, and it is beautiful beyond all imagining."

A Red Indian once spoke these words:

"There is a sweet home where wondrous beauties await you. That home is my portion now. I have gone on beyond this; excuse me saying so, but it means coming back to get into your surroundings.

There are sheltering arms outstretched to shield and guard you and those who are dear to you, bearing them up with supplication and prayer, and we will do the best we can for you all the way. It is one of the Indian Chiefs who brings this message to you. You know something of the power of what you call prayer, but it has much more wonderful power than you realise, so you know what to do."

The power of the mind for good, creates our comfort and happiness in the hereafter, as a Scottish friend once put it:

"The glittering gowd (gold) is no good here, but the glittering gowd of the heart—duties done in earth life, they stick to you. Even the smallest acts of kindliness count. A pat on the back, a few words of cheer to a weary traveller on the way, these cost nothing but mean so much. God bless you. I am just an old-timer from the spirit side of life, looking for the weary wanderers on the plane of earth, where I did some weary wandering in the old times past, wishing to give them a pat on the back now and again, and by doing so I get a blessing myself, Aye, Aye.

A banker present was once addressed in these words:

"It is also a crown of rejoicing to me, my friend of the money change. I do not know your name, but I know you work with money. It is necessary to your side. You could not go through life without it, but, when you come to my side, you will not require to buy anything. You will have justice according to what you have done in life and done in love, according to what God would wish you to do. Good-bye, good-bye."

The same idea was expressed on another occasion when the same banker was addressed by a friend, in these words:

"There are no balance-sheets on this side, the clinking cash will not buy you anything here. It is amusing to think how some hang on to it so long, and it worries them even on this side because they cannot get using it as they want to do."

Once, during a conversation, I asked if those with earth titles retain them in Etheria, to receive this reply:

"Earth titles mean nothing to us. As soon as those bearing them arrive here these prefixes are dropped, they are meaningless to us."

A lady present once asked her husband in the other world if he and their son were together. His reply also embraced another theme:

"Very often, but, of course, we are not together always. You will find my voice quite different now to what it used to be in days of old. You will find when you get to this side of life and can be with the beautiful friends that I have met, you will take on other accents. You are marching through a weary world which is coming through a terrible time, and it is your duty, as far as you can, to live as you know God would wish you to." (This remark refers to the Second World War.)

This subject of the human voice was raised on another occasion, when a lady present asked a friend in Etheria if one with a beautiful voice on earth would have one in the other world. This was the reply:

"One with a beautiful voice will continue to have a beautiful voice on the spirit side, but a beautiful voice can be cultivated here, even if you did not have one in the body, and, with a beautiful voice, anyone can sing, and sing beautifully, and you acquire all these things very quickly."

Music was then discussed. A lady present asked if there was music in the world from which her friend was speaking:

"Every sort of music you wish, you can hear. There are many choirs who sing here, just the same as you sing on the Earth Plane."

A young woman present one evening heard her name spoken by a voice claiming to be that of an uncle on the other side. His remarks emphasise the natural friendly way in which they live together:

"I met an old friend of yours—a very dear friend of yours; you ken (know) Jimmie. I have made his acquaintance and he is keeping fine and always thinking about you. By the by, when the course is run with you all, it is then you will pick up all your old friends you knew in the old days, and all faults, all follies and forgetfulness will be wiped out, and you will be happy together. Now, good night, and be happy, my dear."

Another glimpse of their way of life comes to us in the remark a lady in the other world once made to a lady friend present at the meeting:

"I have not only seen your dear husband but I have spoken to him many a time."

Once we were told of one way they make new friends, and this was not the first time I had heard about it. Just as happens on earth, when people make new friends at these little Spiritualist meetings, so they do likewise in Etheria when people gather together to converse with us on earth. Many new acquaintances are made in this way. What follows was said to a lady present by her mother on the other side, after the mother had made some outspoken remarks about a person they were discussing:

"I was always outspoken and said what I thought about things, and I am still the same. I have also made many friends here whom I never met until I came here—such as Mrs. McRobbie, and others I have met through coming into contact with them at these Meetings. But, oh, darling, I do miss you very much."

Mrs. McRobbie is the mother in Etheria of one of the lady sitters.

A lady present was told this by her granduncle who has spoken to her on many occasions:

"It is now David speaking again. I want you to understand that your Mother is 'in the pink'. Excuse the expression, but why should I not say 'in the pink'? And I hope you are too."

One who was noted for his humour on earth gave this reply to a question asked by a gentleman present:

"Thank you, Sir. Yes, I had, and have yet, a good sense of humour."

No sooner was this said than an Irishman in Etheria, a relation of one of the ladies present, ejaculated in the Irish brogue:

"Faith, and it was not half so good as mine, you know. It is Brian speaking."

On another occasion Brian returned, and, after saying something, he laughed. A lady said it was nice to hear his cheery laugh. To this he replied:

"Sure, I laugh. Why should I not laugh? The world is full of sorrow, but why should those who

feel like laughing not smile? Always remember that a smile from you may lessen the sorrow of some weary soul."

A humorous remark, once made by another Irishman, caused all present to laugh heartily, and then he was heard to say:

"Sure it is quite cheery to hear your laughter. I like to hear you laugh like that."

The grandfather of the husband of a lady present, in the course of conversation once made this rather flattering remark about himself. He was evidently no puritan in his outlook on life:

"You did not know him in earth life, and you would get a great surprise if you could see him now, and compare him with that old photograph you were speaking about. He is a much more handsome man now. Are you laughing at my vanity? I like to say cheerful things and make you laugh. If I could not be happy and joyous when I come back to earth conditions, I would not come at all. Clean joy and clean pleasure are part of God Himself. Had you been all the time, what you call years, on this side that I have been, and got such great help from those who have progressed further, you would be joyous and glad too. I was never a grumbler, and as far as we are doing the Master's Will (keeping within the law), we can travel about and do what we like."

The subject of fun, humour, and enjoyment on the other side was once summed up in these few words by an Etherian after he had made an amusing remark to a lady present:

"We are pretty natural on this side of life, as you

will find out when you come over here. I find it so anyhow."

One who gave his name and claimed to be the author of that name, one of outstanding fame during the latter part of the 19th century, once spoke these words:

"If you cannot make the pathway trod in earth life brighter for those who follow, you have failed much in your duty. You have all something to give, and I am sure you will endeavour to give of your best that those who follow after may say: 'She did it well,' or 'He did it well.' Do so, my friends. Do so, my dearest friends. What a record to carry with you. God bless you."

On another occasion a gentleman present, who had done much good for mankind, was told:

"Your garments will shine with a greater brilliance and place you in the 'Advance Guard', girt with the armour of righteousness, for all you have done to help those stragglers by the way as you go through life. Those records cannot be hid when you come to this side. You will bear the imprint of your actions in earth life, and those which are good will help you all the better when you come to this side of life—every one of you. See, then, that you do all the good you can, while you can. Life is real and unending. It is merely a changing scene from one phase to another."

And, with the change, earth's worries cease, as we were told:

"God bless you. It will be a happy day when all earth worries are over and all meet again on the other side of life. I do not mean to hurry any of you away, but you will tune yourself in on the spirit side of life, each one of you, when you come over, and renew again the friendships with those you used to meet in the earth surroundings."

From what they say it would seem that worry, care and anxiety, which we associate with life, is absent from them. Doubtless they have troubles of their own about which we know nothing, but this is what we were told:

"I am sure, the way you all have to go, each and every one of you has your varied worries and anxieties, but trust to those who have gone before. They will help you and they will look after those you love who are away from you. The path which you have to tread on earth, do so with steadfast steps, firm and true; an example to those who falter by the way, remembering always there may be a weaker brother taking an example from you, lest you detract from the straight path that leads to the light. Keep the light ahead, and the course straight, and the goal will come in sight when all you love so well will be with you, and eternal peace."

This cessation of worry, such as everyone experiences in earth life, was emphasised again on another occasion in these words:

"You will find a difference when you come to our side. All the tangled skeins will be unravelled, and you will have no more worry about anything."

A lady present was once told by her grandfather:

"I know how hard the little worries pinch at times. There are some worries which are met with on life's road that are gie (very) difficult to deal with, but, remember, the corner is not far away. Take it from me, you cannot see round and it is a case of contemplating what is round the corner. What is round the corner will be very bright for you, my lassie. I must watch you with the greatest care, but I am afraid I am taking up too much time. The atmosphere in this home to-night is very congenial to me."

Earth worries will cease, but nevertheless they have their regrets for past mistakes. This is what was once said by a father in Etheria when speaking to his daughter:

"I regret all my mistakes. We have made many of them as we go through life. We all make blunders, but I find myself in a very happy condition here. I am only anxious about those I left behind."

Many of our regrets, worries, and anxieties on earth come from our own folly and stupidity. Here is the message of one on the other side, giving us advice gained from his own experience:

"Pardon me, but I think I heard one of you speaking about the privilege of having your own ideals and ideas. Well, I would just like to say that it is also good to listen to other people's opinions and ideas as one walks along the path of life. Try to see through your brother's spectacles clearly, and then the world may seem a little different to you. I am speaking to no one in particular but to all of you, and to myself.

"When I was in the body I had no opinion but my own, and I was right, of course. How foolish that seems to me now. I am speaking about my earth life, of course, but now that has passed away. I am sorry for disturbing you, but I came in and I like to look at your faces. I can see you all perfectly, and when I come close to you I see you better. I see the darkness of shadow around some of you, and the bright light around others, but I know that the shadow which is over some of you (Second World War), and it seems rather overbearing, is caused by worry over those you love. Do not worry overmuch."

To conclude this subject of worry and regrets, let me give the remark of one who claimed to be an old friend of someone present:

"Let the light shine in your souls, and you will see the beauty of all the beauties which are around about you. We all make mistakes, but our mistakes purify us sometimes, at least they purify our outlook. I hope I am not intruding by putting my thoughts before you."

That their thoughts produce their clothes seems evident from what we were once told by an Etherian. This power, which mind has over matter in Etheria, is difficult for us to grasp. They tell us that they have the power to mould etheric matter as they think. Consequently, their houses are the products of their minds. As they think, they construct. This was clearly told me on more than one occasion. So, when we are told what follows about their clothes it may be difficult to understand, but it all fits in with what they have said to us at different times about their production and constructive methods.

We have the same mind in Etheria as we have on earth, or, to be more exact, we *are* the same mind there as here, and, when we think what our mind does here, we can believe it is possible for it to have even more extensive power in the other world. Before our conscious mind took control, our subconscious mind had fashioned tubes for conducting our blood, a pump we call the heart, to pump our blood continuously through our arteries and veins every day for some sixty-eight years of the average civilised individual's lifetime. Before the conscious mind of man had discovered how to make metal pumps, tubes, levers, etc., the subconscious mind had directed their construction in flesh and bones in the human body, so what is it not capable of doing in a world of finer matter where its control is so much greater?

I try to liken the human mind to a tree. We see and sense its leaves and branches, which can be compared to the conscious mind. The unconscious mind can be compared to its roots, the unseen life-giving part of the tree, from which comes its form and vitality. What is visible appeals to us, but not the invisible, and so with our mind, the conscious part being like the visible tree but the unconscious very real mind like the vital roots which nourish the tree. After death the subconscious mind of earth seems to become more prominent, to rise and give visible expression such as it does not do on earth. It is here, in the subconscious, that the power of the mind lies, and, when its potency is released, to become more visible after death, much will be possible for us to do that we cannot do on earth.

This is what we were once told by an Etherian at the close of a long talk:

"I have progressed since then, and now I am able to return to the surroundings of earth life and be clothed in apparel like what I used to wear. The clothes change. I cannot tell you how, but, as we draw near the physical, the clothes change, there is no doubt about it. Perhaps I have not put it very clearly to you, but, when I draw near to the Earth Plane, I find myself standing in the surroundings where I used to stand, with similar garments to those I used to wear in earth life, and the robes I wear on the other side of life—the Summerland side—change, imperceptibly to me, when I cross the border through the mist. Of course, there are others who can come, more advanced than I am, and they always come in their spirit robes. I wish you could see them —they are very beautiful."

Their minds have not only supernormal power over substance, but they also seem to have the power of transferring thoughts from mind to mind without the use of speech. They do use the spoken word just as we do, but they have a telepathic gift which is very rare and exceptional on earth. This is what I was once told in answer to a question I asked about the different languages spoken in Etheria:

"There are the various earth languages spoken here, such as English, French and German, but they are conveyed from mind to mind mentally. Communication takes place mentally from one to another, not only by the spoken word as on earth. This is just as if I were to say that the mind of the spirit gets into telepathic touch with the mind with which he is communicating."

A lady present asked her mother in Etheria if she had met Aunt Agnes, to be told:

"No, but I have spoken to her, just as you would talk to someone on the 'phone. It is not the same, but that is the only way I can describe it. When I get the condition, I am able to speak to her. She is on beyond me. You will get many surprises at what happens here."

A man in Etheria who said he was not far advanced, in fact, that he was rather backward, confirmed this telepathic form of communication which all understand, no matter what was their earth language, because the pictures formed in one mind are conveyed to the one with which it is in communication. This is what he said:

"I do not want to go very far on my way until I get the members of my own family with me. Meantime I understand that once we pass beyond these spheres in which I have been for a very long time, we shall at once acquire the knowledge of a language which everyone knows."

This greater freedom of expression, their greater ease of travel, their immense mental power over matter, may be the reason for the greater harmony which there prevails. This remark was once made in the course of a long conversation between the sitters and an active friend and helper on the other side:

"There will be no unification of the peoples of the world until they all reach this plane of life, where no enmity, no jealousy or hatred to anyone can intervene. That is what I meant by unification, and then all will be well for all, but, until that time, be up and doing, by prayerful thoughts and kindly deeds, to help to bring comfort and cheer to the lonely ones."

When reading the next chapter, it will be evident that they are generally delighted to get into contact once more with friends on earth. In spite of the difficulties they experience in communicating with us, they face it with a will and determination because, as we were once told by one of our friends there:

"It is a great satisfaction to us to know that the little thoughts, which we have managed to give of our knowledge of life here, are acceptable to you. Thank you very much. You will find when you come to my side that there was so much you could have done in earth life if you had just opened your heart. I am not speaking to you personally, you know, at all. I am just voicing the thoughts which are in my soul from my own experience."

So let us now proceed with another phase of this all-embracing subject.

CHAPTER XI

THEIR CONTACT WITH US

THE evidence we received of the interest and affection which Etherians have for us on earth did not come from a series of questions and answers, but by the remarks they made from time to time, often in the course of conversation. When these are all brought together it is evident that in many cases their memories of earth life are as vivid as they were when they lived on earth, and that their interest in their friends, and affection for their relations still on earth, is as strong as it ever was.

Besides the remarks they made, the tone of their voices conveyed, as much as their words, their pleasure in being able to speak to us on earth. To be able to tell us of the fact that they still live and love, that they are happy and eagerly awaiting the time when their relations will join them, gave them intense pleasure.

So let us read their varied remarks on their contact with us, which is the subject of this chapter.

A young man who had met a tragic death once spoke to a friend amongst the sitters. After giving his name, he said these words in the course of a general conversation:

"It is so delightful to be beside you. It is not every day I get a chance of sending a message. I am thinking about my beloved friend, Mary Stope. God bless her for her friendship to me. It is all fresh to me when I come back and look at you all. I have passed the way by which all come. You are filing past the milestones, my friends, Ladies and Gentlemen. I went over before I had passed many milestones. I have come to such a wonderful country, and I have got such wonderful work to do."

A lady present once heard her sister's voice. First of all the sister gave her name, and then said this in reply to the hope expressed that she is now happy after all her earth's sorrows:

"My earth sorrows are as nothing to me now. I am glad to be away from it all. I am so happy here. I love you, darling, and will do all I can to help you and keep you company, for you are lonely sometimes.

"And now I am going to help you, dear, all I can. Isn't it fine that we can speak to each other, and that you got to know about this ?"

A mother in Etheria once told her daughter this, in reply to a question as to whether or not she was happy in her new life:

"I just wish you were half so well and happy as I am ; all my worry is to see you worried and nobody with you. I would not come back, darling, but I am so glad to come and talk to you. I would rather stay here, and get everything very nice for your homecoming."

Those who spoke to us often referred to their happiness, but this is sometimes tempered with sadness for the friends and relations they have left behind, if they are unhappy and lonely. Happiness in Etheria is also affected by the general misery on earth caused by strife and suffering. As one of them once expressed it during the Second World War:

"You know, sweet lady, there are so many in trouble today on your side of life. I tread the path of your earth way at times and my heart is sad. I know you are wondering at me saying 'My heart is sad', but I take on the feelings of sadness, distress and sorrow which are around, and I just wish I could lift them all away. I just wish all on the Earth Plane could get into harmony with divine love and leave their cares and sorrows behind them."

Another Etherian once put it this way:

"I wonder myself when I look back on those whom I loved and still love who are coming through such trying times (Second World War), and I cannot do anything but pray that you may be assisted and supported through it all, though I know you will be compensated for it all. There are very few to-day who have not their own particular worry or care. I think you know what I mean, just that little care and heartache that you can tell to no one but yourself and your spirit friends; and I, although I have not exactly earned the right to call you my friends, am eager and willing to help you in every way I can. I know there are others over me who are ready to help you."

During a long conversation with a lady present, an Etherian, who claimed acquaintance with her son in Etheria, once spoke as follows:

"I have traversed a great many spaces since coming to this side of life, and I thank the great Spirit God for allowing me to have that great joy and privilege. I have now been appointed to operate on your Earth Plane for some considerable time, trying to alleviate the sadness and take away the sorrows of those who are on the Earth Plane needing help. I try to help those who are grieving for dear ones through this war, and impress upon them that there are myriads of souls who come to alleviate the suffering of those who are passing through war to this side of life. They do so by taking the consciousness away. I will stand aside now, Ladies and Gentlemen, for a little while, but with your permission I may come in again later if I get the opportunity."

Another amplified the foregoing at another séance in these words:

"We are not sad—quite the reverse; it is only when we see and feel the unhappiness of others on contacting your plane that we take on a kindred feeling. You would not be human if you did not feel sad and sorrowful for others at times. We would not be brothers and sisters to each other if we did not get this mutual sorrow, and this applies not only to your friends, but to all those ministering angels who watch over you. They have kindred feelings with you, and enter into all your sorrows and all your joys, and try to help you at all times."

A lady present on another occasion heard this said at the close of a short talk she had with one who had been in love with her when he was on earth:

"It is so nice to see you. So nice to hear you say we will meet again. There are no jealousies here. We all love one another and help each other—both here and on your plane—and I will help you all I can."

A recently widowed lady once received this message about her husband:

"He is happy and cheerful and wants you to try and be happy too. There are many friends here who are interested in you, and they want you to know that though they do not speak to you they are close, and will all be looking after you."

Once, after a hymn had been sung to relieve any tenseness amongst the sitters, there came clearly the name and voice of a woman, a friend of most of the sitters, who had passed on some months previously:

"Oh, do sing it again, my darlings! I love to hear you sing and I love to join in these hymns. It brings back the old days when I was in the body."

Undoubtedly their coming to these séances brought back their earth memories. A friend in Etheria once said this to a lady:

"I can see you all. I can see you just as you are sitting in that chair, and apparelled just as I had clothes in earth life. I see your hair has a beautiful curl and you have a nice complexion."

A son, who often came back and spoke to his mother, a regular sitter, once said these words. He has been previously referred to as a teacher in one of their universities:

"My Mother, we are both beside you, sweet Mother, Father and I. I have stood in silence listening to the beautiful heartfelt words that friend—that Indian friend—spoke just now, and I felt my heart rejoice that my labours on this side have been of some use because he is one of my pupils. Oh, that I could draw the curtain aside and portray the beautiful picture to you of what is to come! We are not able to do so. There are certain things you are not allowed to know until you join us here. It is an amazing time we are living in, dear friends, just now. Mother dear, I am just looking at you."

The father in Etheria of a lady present had once a talk with his daughter, which concluded with these words:

"Mother and I hope you will have a very happy time for the remainder of your earth career, and we will be standing at the gateway awaiting you when God's good time comes. God bless you, my beloved lassie. You have had a chequered life lately, we know. I mean ups and downs, and you are missing us very much now, me and Mother. You took great care of Mother, and now I have her here to take care of, and I think you will understand, my dear, when I say that I think I understand her even better than you."

When a mother present asked her son in Etheria if he had been with her when she had been from home he replied:

"And so I was, Mother dear, and I am with you now. I am with you many times when you don't know it, when you are not thinking about me. I know that you think about me often; but often, when you are not, I am beside you, helping you out of your difficulties, because you have difficulties, sometimes, dear, and you wonder often how things have smoothed out as they do."

At the end of a long conversation between a mother in Etheria and her daughter who was present at the séance, the mother remarked:

"I would just surprise you if you could see me standing beside you."

A schoolmaster present was once told this in a conversation with a lady in Etheria, at whose house, when she was on earth, he had séances in the Ayrshire village of West Kilbride;

"It is such a wee world when you come to think about it. Here I am on the other side of life, in the new world, and yet I can come, just by thought, practically instantly to see you as I used to see you in the old days at West Kilbride."

During a conversation that a boy in Etheria was having with his mother, he addressed all present in these words, which make clear the pleasure it is to our friends on the other side to come again in contact with those they love on earth:

"It is such a joy to me, friends, to speak to my Mother like this. When I found I could do so, it was a great joy to me, and I have tried to help others to get the joy of speaking to those they love on the Earth Plane. It makes me very happy to talk to you and try to help you."

This is what was told to a lady present by her mother in Etheria. After giving her name and referring to her daughter by name she went on:

"It is Mother speaking, and it is just like yesterday since you were a wee prattling thing running about my feet. God bless you, my dear. You are toddling down the hill now."

The words which follow greatly comforted a widow who was present; they were spoken to her by her husband. If other widows could be as sure as she is that their husbands are awaiting them, how much needless sorrow and mourning would cease on earth!

"Norman is speaking to you. My dear, how do you do? I am away at the other side of the room so that I can amplify my voice a little better for you. It is not tuned in yet as I would like it to be. The love which is in our souls, my dear, is still burning strong, and, as your days run past, I am watching you. God bless you. I will never be properly happy until we shake hands and clasp each other when God's good time comes. In the interval I will guard you to the best of my ability, as far as the spirit friends who guide me here allow me to do so."

Marriage on earth can either be happy, fairly happy, or unhappy. Marriage, as we understand it on earth, does not exist in Etheria, but those who love each other come together again when both reach the other side. The fairly happily married people generally remain friends, and the unhappily married see little or nothing of each other. The happily married here have been fortunate in each finding a mate on earth, but those less fortunate will some time find a partner in Etheria to their liking, if there is harmony between them and they are congenial to each other. This briefly is what I have been told from the other side, and it seems reasonable, natural, and what we might expect from the knowledge we have of the way they live.

A gentleman, who was a regular sitter, had many talks with his wife on the other side. Once, after assuring her of his constant affection for her, she replied:

"I know, Don. We are twin souls in many things. You know what I mean, and the great mystery of life is—I had to leave you sooner than I would have liked. You have been so brave, Donald, and you have been so good to your charges left in your care. There have been some little things that have worried you, but I am always helping you,

Donald. Good day. At the end of the road, my dear, when the good Spirit God will call you home, Mary will be waiting there."

All kinds of men, women, and children of the other world visited the Sloan circle over a period of about forty years, and many hundreds of earth visitors were welcomed by the regular sitters. These visitors received ample evidence that those they thought of as dead were really alive and, though now unseen, loved them as they did when they lived on earth. Thousands of evidential messages were given which proved the identity of those who spoke, but most of them are lost because they were never put in writing.

It is from those séances that were recorded, that the extracts given in this book are taken, but I have omitted all references to evidence of identity, and mentioned personal names as seldom as possible. This book is of an educational nature, and is confined to what they tell us about the world in which they live and their life there. Evidence of identity was always freely given, and this will be found in some of my other books.

What the pages of this book contain are of interest to everyone, whereas evidence of identity can only completely convince the individual who receives it. All the speakers, whose words are here recorded, fully satisfied their friends on earth by the intimate things they said, that they were none other than the personalities they claimed to be. So I think that what else they said, besides the proofs they gave of their identity, can also be accepted.

On the other hand, if we reject the personalities behind the voices which spoke, how are we to account for them, and all they told us? Behind a voice must be a body to vibrate our atmosphere, and behind the body a brain which is controlled by an individual mind. Everything recorded is too immense to be the product of a human fraud, intent on deceiving his fellow creatures. Everything is too consistent, too patently genuine, and too impossible for the ordinary intelligence to imagine as planned deceit and fraud.

Sloan was tested in every possible way, and he was not the only direct voice medium in the world. There are, and have been, many others, and these conversations between the two worlds, both evidential and informative, have been going on for the past hundred years in many parts of the globe. They have been taking place wherever there was someone who could supply the people on the other side with ectoplasm to enable them to materialise their vocal organs. It is unfortunate that only a comparatively few of these séances have been recorded, to be handed down to future generations.

Throughout all these records there is a consistency in everything said, the same descriptions of Etheria, the same way of life reported, the same assertion that it is how we live that is important, and not what creeds we believe. This is so uniform, and yet so contrary to the orthodox religious teaching accepted by the majority of mankind, that its consistency cannot be the product of earth minds widely separated throughout the world.

Moreover, what they tell us contradicts the materialistic orthodox teaching of death and the resurrection. In fact, the views they express so revolutionise orthodox religious thought throughout the world, that theologians and ecclesiastics have nothing better to put forward than that the devil is behind it all, for the purpose of creating more and more unbelievers in the generally accepted religion.

After this digression, we shall now return to our conversations, and relate what was said to a hospital nurse by a doctor friend in Etheria. After telling the nurse that he had been with her at an operation that day at a certain hospital which he correctly named, he went on to say how much pleasure it gave him to help earth doctors and nurses to heal the sick and suffering. To this effort, he said, he gave much of his time and, after receiving the nurse's thanks, he replied to her, and then spoke to all present in the circle:

"Mine is the pleasure, Miss Duff. It is so nice, friends, to know and realise when you come to this side of life, if you have not realised it previously, that you can still be in touch with what interested you in earth life, by getting into contact with, and speaking to, those whom you knew before, letting them know that life on earth is not the end of your journey. It is just the beginning of that perfect day which you find when you come to my side. May God bless, comfort, and cheer you in these troublous times, may He cheer those who weary and wait for loved ones they will never see again in the physical; many of them without your knowledge of the bright future awaiting them. It is up to you who know and understand, who have the Light, to pass it on to others."

An Etherian once spoke to a lady present. She asked who was speaking, and he replied:

"You do not know me. I know your son, Mr.

Arthur Lang, very well; not in earth life, you know, but after coming over. I had been over for many years before Mr. Lang, but I got to know him here and I do like him very well."

"Can you tell us something about yourself?" she then asked, to which he replied:

"I may stay and look on. I like to hear others speaking, those that are on my side, as well as those on your side. I love to hear your voices talking to each other. I was not an educated man in earth life; what you would call an educated man, but I have learned a great deal since coming over here. I hope you will understand if I put it in my own phraseology and say: there are many different spheres, many different stages of existence on the spirit side of life."

On another occasion, someone on the other side showed the same interest in what was going on at the séance:

"I am just a stranger. I saw the lights. They attracted me, and I came in to see if I could be of any little service to any one of you, dear friends. I would rejoice if my own dear ones knew that it was possible for me to contact them and speak to them, but they know nothing of this. I speak to them sometimes, but they do not hear me. How wonderful it is that you hear me. May God the Father lead you to the light that will keep the door still open for you to pursue this truth right along your way of life until the journey ends. Do your level best to keep a clean record and you will have a joyful entrance into spirit life when your time comes."

After an interesting discourse, which has been recorded in a previous chapter, an Etherian finished his conversation with a gentleman present with these words:

"And now, my friend, I must go. I have been trying to explain in my humble way what I felt in my own soul in the spirit side of life, and the progress from one stage to another. It is not all known in a day.

"It is a slow process, and those of us who work near the Earth Plane, I do not know just how to put it to you, I do not mean to say that we deteriorate in any way, but we have rather given up of our own accord our advancement for a little while, that we may help our weaker brothers, as we ourselves have been helped in the past. We do not stay near the Earth Plane, but we come and work in it. I think that none of you present would regret a little time given to help a backward brother or sister into a higher level of life. I must go. I am called now by an emissary of one of the Shining Ones, into a higher level of life."

A regular helper on the other side, who spoke clearly and often, sometimes at great length, made the following observations in the course of a long talk:

"I would like to make a pathway clear for you Ladies and Gentlemen, to tread the devious paths of life, which just now is a very difficult matter. It comes hard to the human heart. I am speaking more like one of yourselves to-day. I am trying hard to enter into your sorrows and your joys, and to assist the friends you love who may be passing just a little ahead of you on the road of life. I try to bear you up in the arms of love, to bear you up beyond the shadow to the substance where I live, and where some day you will be co-partners in the labour of love."

At another time a Red Indian, who often came to help newcomers to speak, expressed the same sentiments in these words:

"I have tried both in earth life and spirit life to bring joy and cheer to both sides. You know what I mean, to comfort and soothe the sorrowful ones. The blessing of the Indian Chief goes with you all."

It was natural that those whose minds retained memories of their earth life, and who had friends still on earth, would be the ones who took the most trouble to come and speak to us. They live on the planes within closest touch of the earth. Nevertheless, things take place on earth which escape their notice, as happened with this lady when her daughter on earth asked her if she had met a friend recently passed over:

"Oh, darling, I did not know he was here. Do take my love to them. Be sure and say it came from this side. It has just been veiled from me for a little while, but I will try and get in touch with him now that I know."

On another occasion their limitations were expressed in these words:

"Anything done by friends in the earth life who have erred, if it would hurt those who love them who have gone before, a veil is thrown across, that they do not know about it. If it is conducive to their happiness this veil will be thrown, and they will not be permitted in the surroundings if it is going to make them sad and hamper their progress on this side of life."

Another Etherian who was standing by took up the theme in these words:

"Had I lived a better life in the material I would not have been so sad when I first came over here. That was a beautiful illustration of a veil being drawn so that dear ones on this side do not always know what is going on among their friends on earth. It is only the grosser things that are hidden from them. I hope you will understand. I am a very plain fellow and I am only putting my own thoughts through, which I have gathered from experience, and which I know to a great extent to be true on this side."

With a slight pause he continued his talk:

"We only know to a limited extent what is going on on the Earth Plane. Those in the high planes—the Ministering Angels and the Shining Ones—do, however, know all, and shade certain things off that would spoil the happiness of those on this side. Certainly this veiling-off helps you in the earth life; in your case with regard to the future. If you had known beforehand the trials you would have to come through (Second World War) you would not have had the strength to go on. It is better that a veil should also be drawn on the material side of life. Place, therefore, your trust in God, and do the right."

Another slight pause was noticed, and then he continued, every word said being clearly delivered without the least hesitation:

"With regard to what was said about certain things being veiled off on this side; you might have a gentle spirit on this side of life—I am speaking to you all in general—someone you loved very much and who had always led a very sheltered life. Well, you would not like her progress here to be barred by any mistakes you made. Such as these do not know details of any wrongdoings or sorrow. They, however, sense immediately when anything goes wrong with you, and will help you all they can with their thoughts of love and their prayers; for we remember here those we love, just as you do. We know instinctively when you are in a tight corner, even if we do not know details, and then you are influenced by our prayers for you."

A lady present was once asked by a friend on the other side to convey his affection to his wife on earth. Addressing the lady by her pet name he said:

"Tell Annie I love her still. My passing has not broken the link between us. Oh, my dear, oh, it is wonderful. It is James speaking. It is wonderful that we can come in here, and that I have managed. I was just afraid that I would not be able to make myself heard, and I have stood beside you for that purpose. I am well, and oh, so happy, though, of course, I have my cravings for some I have left behind. You know what I mean, but I am working all I can to let those I have left have peace and happiness. It is so difficult (because of the war)."

An aunt of a lady present once came back and was delighted that she was able to touch her niece.

"It is a nice feeling to know that I can touch you and that you know I am here. Think of me sometimes, and I will do the best I can for you, and I will look after the boys."

She stated correctly that she had died a year and a few days before her niece was born. Then followed a talk between them about two relations still on earth. The niece then felt a hand touching her, the aunt's concluding words being:

"This is just the touch of a vanished hand, a hand you never knew in earth life touches you now."

The same sitter on a previous occasion was told this by her husband's grandfather. Replying to a remark she made, he continued:

"Yes, and I am so glad to have got this first word with you. I shall come again, God willing. Peace be with you all, and all those who have not got the great privilege of the knowledge you have. Let the whispering words of truth penetrate their minds, and say: 'We are not dead, we are alive.' Adieu."

On another occasion, the mother of a lady present (who had passed on when her daughter was a small child) said to her daughter:

"Mother never forgets. I watched you while you grew up, studied your little ways. I am your Mother. I have opened my arms and I hold you. God bless you, darling. What I can do for you, I will. All will be done for you to the very utmost. I was present at one or two tragic episodes in your life and I held on to you, especially at one time when you were very low down."

When a sitter once remarked how wonderful it was, and how happy the sitters should be to have their friends from the other world coming to speak to them, someone from that world spoke these words:

"When we love someone then nothing is a trouble; nothing is too much and no work too tedious to bring joy to those we love. This, however, is not tedious work, but a great joy to us, getting these little messages through to you."

How close the thought link is between the people of the two worlds was once emphasised during a talk between a gentleman present and a friend on the other side.

"There is one thing I can tell you—if you think fondly of someone you loved in the earth life who has gone from you—thought carries here and we get it immediately."

Then the Etherian made an interesting remark in reply to a question:

"Forgetting things you have been told, or taught, is purely a physical thing. You do not forget anything you are taught on the spirit side of life."

That love binds the people of the two worlds together is emphasised by the remark made to us all by the grandfather in Etheria of a lady present:

"I would like just to say to you all, you are very dear to me and dear to others in the spirit side of life, because you help us, when we come to the borderline, to get into touch with those whom we love. Without your help that wee (small) door would remain steekit (shut) and unopened. You ken what I mean. It is the blending of the thoughts, the sympathy received, that lifts the latch and enables us to get through to you and let you know that we still live—still love you. God bless you."

On another occasion when this subject was mentioned we were told to remember that:

"Love is something which is branded on the heart of humanity and can never be eradicated. It lives through all eternity, it never dies, the love which is

in the heart for each other grows brighter all the time."

This theme was touched on at another séance when a lady present was speaking to her mother in Etheria. "Mother," she said, "will you give my love, dear, to the one who tried to take your place?" Her mother replied:

"I will do so. It is easy to pass on love. There is no thought of jealousy now. It is only love we can give. We could not convey anything other than love. There could be no message conveyed to anyone on this side if it was not a message of love. God bless you."

Mr. Edward Clodd, who exposed the superstition in organised orthodox religion, wrote in 1917 that "out of the enormous mass of communications purporting to come from discarnate spirits, not an ennobling or high toned message can be extracted; all, all is nauseating, frivolous, mischievous, spurious drivel". He was an agnostic, being one of the leaders of materialistic thought in the early part of the 20th century, and I do not doubt that this is what he sincerely believed, because he was ignorant of the truth. This hatred and ignorance of everything to do with Spiritualism was shared by the vast majority of his contemporaries, and still is, but to a lesser degree, to this day.

Nevertheless, a considerable amount of literature on the beliefs of Spiritualists was available in his day, to anyone who cared to study it, and it has grown enormously since then. Some day the barrier of prejudice and ignorance will be swept away, and the monotonous clamour of abuse which Spiritualism has received over the past hundred years from Christians and materialists alike will cease.

If everyone possessed psychic gifts, or if everyone had one psychic experience, or more than one, the hard crust of materialism and antagonism would dissolve. The Spiritualist outlook on life, death, and the after life, would take their place. A new, broader, and more complete conception of the meaning of existence would follow, and much present-day sorrow, unhappiness and frustration would cease. In this world, as in the next, there are planes of thought, and those less mentally developed cannot grasp what those with greater knowledge are able to accept. Everything in life is a question of mental development.

There have been in the past the more enlightened who have risen mentally above their fellow men and women, and pierced to a greater or lesser extent the veil which divides the visible from the invisible world. Some have been born with this greater insight, some have been fortunate to have had experiences denied to others, and some people have learned from what the few have had to tell them. However, the enlightenment of the masses will only come as mediumship and learning increase, but, with comparatively few mediums in our midst, progress in the knowledge of what is true can only come slowly.

Meanwhile, let those who read this book try to grasp the wonder of it all, and realise how this knowledge revolutionises much of what we were taught to believe to be true. The revolution in thought it brings about is as tremendous as was the complete change, the reversal of outlook, which took place in the 16th and 17th centuries of our era when, in 1543,

Copernicus, and then Galileo about a hundred years later, with the aid of the newly discovered telescope, revealed the heavens to be something vastly different from what they appeared to be by our ordinary vision.

It took many years even for the intelligent in those days to have an idea of the meaning of it all, and even now our mysterious universe is not within the grasp of human intelligence. The medium which caused this revolution in thought was the telescope, and the medium which is causing the change in our religious outlook is the human being, endowed by nature with a body capable of supplying invisible beings with what they need, to enable them to communicate with us and tell us who they are, and how and where they live.

What a revelation it is, but let me give you the words of an Etherian, who once entered into a conversation we were having with a friend on the other side who had remarked about Mr. Sloan having opened a door for them to get through to us. This is what he said:

"It is a great gift, Mr. Cameron, to be able to open the door, and enable the friends who are around you to exchange thoughts and opinions which may be beneficial to you and to your further progress in life. Whenever you put out a thought, we try to help you in every way we can. You are all friends whom I have met here from time to time, and I have met a goodly number of people of different outlooks on life, but they are all very willing to give an open ear to anything we may say to them, and what we tell seems to be acceptable. We can assure you it is the truth.

"We are only telling you of our own experiences, which we have had since coming to spirit life, and which may help you when the time comes for you to make the crossing to this side of life. That is one thing that makes me very happy, the thought that those on earth life are still able to come and talk to us, and enable us to help you all in the difficult way of life, to help to carry the burden which is near to your hearts and which you may not care to tell to anyone."

This opening up of communication between the two worlds is as much an interest and a delight to them as it is to us on earth. A lady present on one occasion was told this by her father in the other world:

"It is the thought of that great Truth, and the knowledge that you have a perfect understanding of the fact that we still live and love, that helps us to wait with patience for those we love, to join us on this side. We are simply waiting for the day, not longing for it, because to long for that time might shorten the earth life of those we love and long for, but waiting God's good time until the day dawns and the shadows flee away, and we all meet and clasp hands again. When labour is finished, Jordan passed, and life on earth is ended, there is Summer and sunshine and a home of rest at last."

Such words must be a comfort and encouragement to many, but only the few who attend séances with good mediums can have the satisfaction a speaker from Etheria believed was possessed by everyone. He was a Scottish Highlander on earth, and in some of their homes in the highlands the so-called dead and living mingle in a way little realised by the more materialistic lowlanders. The Keltic Highlanders, in remote places, are often highly developed psychically and this is what he said:

"It is not my will that you should not understand it, or not my desire that I should cause you annoyance. I just want to let you know, as I am positive that all of you on earth know already, that those of your loved ones who have gone before are often very near you, and, although you cannot see them, you sense the feeling of their presence, the touch of the hand, the sound of the voice, the loving care of the Mother, and the kind thought of the Father. God bless you, friends."

The touch of the vanished hand is often felt by sitters, as was the case when on one occasion a lady present told us she was being touched on her hands and face. Then we heard:

"It is Mother touching you, and how are you keeping, my dear? I hope you did not hurt yourself much. (She was recovering from a bad fall.) Do you not see Father standing beside you? He is standing just behind you, and I am standing at your left side. I just wish I could throw my arms around you and embrace you properly. It seems a long time now, not so very long, you know, but it seems a long time to me. I am not so very long over, but still I am longing to see my daughter."

On one occasion when the father in Etheria of a lady present was recognised by his daughter, his pleasure was obvious:

"Thank you for recognising me, my beloved daughter. Tell Jim I send him my love, and the whole lot of them. I do not like to disturb them, you know, in their thoughts. It is the truth, and it is a truth that I did not understand very much about myself, and which came as a heavenly revelation to me, when I found that I could come back and speak to you again. I shall never, never leave you until the shadows flee away and the sun rises, and we meet again in the more perfect life and the more perfect world."

Another from Etheria, who spoke in a strong manly voice, once expressed similar sentiments and seemed pleased that the sitters heard what he had to say:

"I do not feel that I am adequately adapted to speak to you, Ladies and Gentlemen, in a way that you ought to be spoken to. It has been a joy and a great upliftment to me to-day that I have been a recipient of the joys and pleasures which you have received in this little Meeting to-night. I have also been uplifted, and my soul has been refreshed and strengthened in the labour of the work which lies before me, by being in your presence to-day. As one who has traversed the Earth Plane long before your time and who has been traversing the planes and spaces for many years, as you count time, I have been in touch time and again with your surroundings, but I have never been able to articulate or speak to you until do-day. To-day I feel uplifted and have joy in the thought that I have got a contact, and I pray that the Great Spirit of Love will allow me to keep in touch with you, to do you some little good from time to time. God bless you all."

In the pause that followed we asked him to give us his name and this is what he said:

"I would not be known to any of you. I am too ancient. By that I mean, it is long as time is counted on the Earth Plane, since I walked there. I did not speak your language, and I did not know your country. I know your language now because I have been deputed to work in your surroundings, and recently have been directed to this gathering to look after you. Do your best to live your earth life as it was intended you should, and a wonderful joy awaits you. There is nothing in God's universe that is not used. He is too wise to have anything that is not necessary. There is a use for everything and a purpose for every one that comes to earth life.

"I will keep in touch with you, and I will come whenever I see that I can be of any service to you and do a little to help. It is always so pleasant and so pleasing for me to give it to you. Adieu."

This desire to help us was also voiced by another male Etherian in these words:

"I should be pleased to help you at any time, any one of you, and, if I cannot answer the questions, I can take them to someone who can illustrate and answer them for you, as far as it is in accordance with the Divine Will. I am not related to any of you in any earth connection, but you are my brothers and sisters, and I am out to help you in any way I can. I do not perhaps know much, but I have gleaned a little knowledge of the theme of the everlasting progress of the human soul towards the Eternal. You understand what I mean."

At another séance a gentleman present remarked that to him the knowledge of human destiny was the greatest interest in life, to hear this reply:

"I understand what you mean, Brother. You just feel when here that you are near those you have loved very much in earth life. You feel you can practically be at one with them."

Then followed a long, intimate talk between him and his wife in Etheria, which ended with these parting words:

"It is a beautiful thought to know that death does not divide us. Just think of the time, dear, when all your efforts and your worries cease, and I and all your friends here welcome you in God's beautiful garden of peace."

Mrs. Sloan, the wife of the medium, passed on in 1940. When on earth she was a regular sitter at these séances, and after her passing she soon came back to become a frequent communicator. She was a woman of a sweet and lovable nature, and this can be realised from the things she said from her new home in Etheria. Mr. Sloan was never paid for the sittings he gave, and considered his part in them as a duty to his friends, but, as he grew older and more feeble, they were certainly a tax on his failing strength.

I am sure he would have ceased giving them in his old age but for one thing, Mrs. Sloan, or Mammy as she was called by some, invariably came back to talk to him and her friends on earth. This fact made life worth living for him, and here are some extracts of what she said on one occasion. First of all she sang a favourite hymn, every word distinct, and led the sitters in the circle, who had only a hazy idea of the words.

Then she said:

"This is Mammy speaking to you. How beautiful

it is just to be in the little circle once again. I can still enjoy it as I did in the days gone by when I met you at these little Meetings from time to time. God bless you, Mrs. Bowes, and those you love. May God support them in the strenuous work and strenuous ways of life just now, and O Father, if it be Thy will, bring this fighting to an end and bring the loved ones home again. Bring harmony and peace once more to this troubled world.

"This is Mammy's prayer to the Great Father God. May He bless your boys, Mrs. Bowes, and may He keep them safe, and may peace and prosperity and the love of God be with you at all times. You were always such a good friend of Daddy and mine, and God bless you, Crissie, my dear. You were always so kind and good to me, and to my dear old man. I wish I could do something to repay you for all your goodness. I thank you one and all for coming here, and standing by my dear old man.

"He is not alone. I tell him often when I am talking to him that he will never be alone while Nanna (Mrs. Sloan's name) is with him.

"I think, Mr. Cameron, that most of us have one or two that are all the world to us. I am afraid I am a wee bit general in my way of thinking, because there were many in the earth life that I loved very fondly, and they are just like all the world to me. It is such a delight to me to be able to come near to them again, and, my dear, dear old man, I am never far away from you. God bless you, Crissie. God bless you, Miss Dearie, and God bless you, my dear old man."

That evening she had much more to say, and her

remarks will be found in their appropriate places. Here in this chapter we are considering what our friends on the other side had to say regarding their contact with us.

A lady schoolteacher, who was sometimes one of the sitters, once received the following message from her mother:

"Isobel—Mamma is speaking. You know all my friends. Remember me to them all, Isobel, and all my love to you, darling."

A Scottish minister, whose church a lady present attended before his death, spoke at these séances from time to time. He never referred to the creeds and doctrines which were the subject of his sermons on earth. Always he dwelt on the importance of righteousness. On this occasion he ended a long discourse with these words:

"Many times, although you do not see the friends, they are helping you from day to day as you travel on, and blessing and guiding you on your way, although you do not know it."

Some of the sitters had sons or relations abroad during one period of the Second World War, and one evening in the course of conversation between the two worlds this is what was said:

"Your friends are all thinking of you. They bear you up, and those of you who have dear ones far away, they are looking after them for you, and they will care for you in every stage of life. It is particularly those who are distant from their home surroundings that I am referring to. There is an ever-watchful eye, in keeping with your prayerful thoughts that crosses space, conveying a loving word, a thought expression, which brings back the sense of home, and comforts them in their lonely times. God bless you."

A Red Indian on the other side, who was well known to most of the sitters present, once remarked:

"Memory is a wonderful thing, a beautiful thing, and it is so nice if you have stored up beautiful thoughts and kind thoughts that you can dwell on afterwards. I have not been here at your Meetings for a little time. I am still interested in you. I know all of you here, and many more who are not here now, but have passed into other scenes, and are watching and guiding your footsteps with loving eyes until you meet again."

This remark led to a general conversation between the two worlds, other Etherians taking part. One was the son of a lady present, and he remarked how nice it was to hold his mother's warm hand. Then he said that his grandfather would speak, and this is what he said:

"It is more wonderful perhaps to us to get the touch of your warm hand, and feel in the actual presence of those we love so well."

Another homely touch came later in the same séance when a relation in Etheria of a lady present replied to a question she asked him. It was: "Had you a painful death, Ikey?"

"No, I am so well now and so happy. Just you think of me as the happy, happy boy that you knew long ago. I will not miss an opportunity of coming to speak to you again. I tried hard to get through. I have to thank Bob for showing me the way. Isaac—I never liked the name Isaac. I liked Ikey better.

You had a nice way of saying it that somehow took the rough edge off it."

Once a regular communicator from the other side, the son of a gentleman present, spoke to a lady in these words:

"Good evening, Mrs. Richardson, I have met you before, but not very often. You have a boy on the spirit side I know, for I saw him standing beside you, although he was not speaking to-night. He went over in a very youthful state, I think."

And then followed a dramatic event, when out of the silence came the cheery voice of this young man who said to his mother:

"Oh, Mother, I am a big strapping fellow now. Can you hear me, Mother? It is just Roy—Roy Richardson."

On one occasion the grandfather in Etheria of a lady present had just spoken to her, when a new voice spoke. This is what we heard:

"I have come down near your plane. It is not your Grandfather speaking now. I just wish to say it is such a delight for all these friends of yours of far-off times when they get into contact with you. I am one of the workers, one of the demonstrators, just doing what I can to hold the doors open and show them the way. Sometimes your friends may be speaking to you and you do not hear them. We do all we can to help by connecting the vibrations."

Once there spoke the voice of one who on earth must have had the psychic gift, though he seemed not to realise how rare it is amongst the people of earth:

"It was in the stillness of the evening, when I was on your Earth Plane, I used to get into some secluded spot in the twilight, delighting in the evening breeze, and listening to the vibrations of those whom I knew were near me somewhere, although I was not physically conscious of their presence. I had the intuition that higher beings than myself were present, and that my immortal soul was being drawn higher towards Heaven, and messages of love, though not in an audible sense, were poured into my heart. That attribute is yours, each and every one of you, so set apart a little time to commune with those you love, and who love you still, although just a little way ahead of you in the road of life. We are all going the same way Home. God bless you."

The conversation once turned to the difficulty most people had in believing in communication with the departed, when a strong man's voice broke in and said:

"When I was in earth life, I could not say I believed it, but I had the consciousness, Ladies and Gentlemen, in my soul that there were people around me, talking to me. I seemed to sense their presence and even to know what they looked like, and, when I came to this side of life, I knew them quite well when they came and spoke to me, and they were not relations at all, but they were friends. A friend is a friend who will always remain a friend if he is a true friend. Well, there are a lot of friends in that sentence."

One of the ladies present once said she regretted not being able to remember her dreams. Then we heard the name of an Etherian, who was well-known to most of the sitters, and this is what he said to a lady present whom he addressed by name:

"I think I might explain a little bit about it. You are often away in your sleep state, and, returning, you know you have met many people on the other side, but you cannot hold these memories or put them in right order. That will come easier by and by. Not so many nights ago you had a very vivid dream of those you love."

Before she could reply, another voice, that of the husband of a lady present, broke in and continued the conversation. His wife replied that she hoped she might meet him in her sleep, and he answered:

"You do not need to hope, my dear; we shall meet. You often meet us in your sleep. I am sure you all know that. You often bring back memories, but they get so jumbled up when you are wakening that you cannot piece them together."

Now we are coming to the end of this long chapter, long because they had always so much to say about their contact with us. They can see and hear us in our every-day life, but we cannot see or hear them except under unusual conditions, and in that way they have an advantage over us. They claim to be able to look after us, but we cannot look after them, and they talk about their contact with us in ways which it is sometimes difficult for us to understand or appreciate. There is more in earth and heaven than most philosophies embrace, and with that let me give you the words of one who once spoke to us in the following poetic strain:

"The spirit of the evening breeze, the spirit whose ears are strained to catch the supplications of those whom they love to answer, to catch the deep call from your heart and succour you, are ever ready to answer that call. There is nothing hid, so you need not fear to tell them all, and, if it is possible, they will help you. We have trod the path before you, we know its roughness, we know the uphill pull, we know how the plain—so clear and smiling—can suddenly be transmuted into a mountain difficult to climb, but be not dismayed, helping hands, beckoning fingers, are near to guide you and help you onwards and onwards."

This chapter can best be terminated by the words of one who often spoke to us, and this is what he once said as he brought a séance to a close:

"My dear friends, I wish I had the power and that I could direct you all into the path of rest, the path of joy, and the path of happiness, but unfortunately, during the earth life you are in, you cannot always take these paths. I have tried to show you the pathway which leads from the cares and troubles of the world life, to rest and peace, to home and friends at last, never more to part again. God bless you."

Finally, these were the words a husband once addressed to his wife:

"I did not get saying good-bye to you, but I will say 'Welcome Home' some day."

She felt the touch of his vanished hand over her face, and the satisfaction she received can also be visualised by those who have their nearest and dearest awaiting them on the other side, as what applied to her applies to all.

CHAPTER XII

THEIR RELIGION

My many friends on the other side seldom spoke about their religious opinions. To them what we call Religion is something very different from what it is to most people on earth. Here on earth we associate religion with saviours, creeds, ceremonials, rituals, churches, mosques, temples, priests and sacred books, but there it is far different. As we progress in Etheria we shall forget the theology we were taught on earth, because we shall find everything is so unlike what most people here are brought up to believe.

What we have been taught is holy and sacred is natural and ordinary. There is nothing sacred or holy in the conversations here reported. We were not speaking to angels, saints, or devils, but to men, women and children who had lived on earth, and are in character much the same now as they were then. The fact that they come to us in a finer body does not change them from being natural into supernatural beings. Now they know that the religious teaching they received on earth was false and the result of theological and mystical imagination. What were ordinary psychic manifestations have been evolved and elaborated into holy and sacred events which all must believe to be saved. Consequently, the people of Etheria pass over those things, which orthodoxy considers of vital importance to mankind, because they have found them to be untrue, unreal, and unrelated to the new life they are now living.

So long as fear and ignorance of the hereafter remain, the orthodox form of religion will continue to be accepted by those whose religious outlook is confined to the traditions of the past. Nevertheless, to rely on the past and try to obtain comfort and enlightenment from ancient sacred writings, while ignoring the greater knowledge of the present, is foolish. Yet the tradition taught to us when our minds were young and plastic is an iron chain which few can break, and the vast majority lean on it as a support to obtain their comfort and religious satisfaction.

Without knowledge of the truth they rely for their salvation on forms and ceremonies, on the repetition of formulae and creeds, on acts of worship, on baptism, eucharists, the last rites and such like, until their church or temple becomes a sacred shrine, and the purveyors of the dogmas and doctrines are considered holy men set apart by God from the rest of mankind.

On one occasion we were talking amongst ourselves at one of Sloan's séances about the ignorance of the clergy concerning psychic matters, when the strong voice of an old friend interrupted our conversation with these words:

"You see, they are bound up so much with their own denominations and the tradition of the Church. They are really in bondage. They are not allowed to teach this truth, although they may acknowledge it in their own souls. It is only sometimes, when they come over to this side of life, and get in touch

with the spiritual side of life, that they waken up, and can do something that helps others."

To only the few has the other world been revealed, and to those who have not been favoured by a psychic experience the crutch of orthodox religion is often a very present help. Anything that helps us to live righteously and to die in peace should not be condemned. Unfortunately, ignorance produces intolerance, and this in the past has caused such persecution and cruelty that the history of many religions, especially the Moslem and Christian, has been so shocking and revolting as to discredit utterly their claims of divine guidance. Twenty-five million victims slaughtered during the Christian era by the Christian church should weigh heavily on the Christian conscience, but it does not because of ignorance of Church history.

When the faithful of every religion reach the other side they naturally expect to find things to be as they believed on earth. Consequently, as they can make their surroundings conform to their thoughts, some believe, as I was once told by an Etherian, that they have actually entered the orthodox heaven. However, as their enlightenment grows these earth beliefs fade away, and they adjust themselves to prevailing conditions.

Instead of what was once to them a sacred mystery, they find themselves in a body similar to their earth body, in a new world very much like the earth they have left, its inhabitants being men, women, and children, actively and usefully employed, and not winged angels forever playing harps and singing praise to God. Consequently, they discover that amongst the intelligent, and those who have been in Etheria for some time, religion is regarded from a different aspect to what it is on earth.

This chapter will make clear how those who spoke at Sloan's séances regard religion, which to us on earth has been as great a force in moulding history as any other factor. At least half the events in history have been caused by religion, and yet, when the mystery and intolerance it caused have been removed, how natural everything is. Then we realise how much suffering, confusion and waste of wealth have come from the ignorance of mankind of what follows death.

Here let me quote the opinion of one who has gone before, and who knows more than do all the mystics, theologians and priests of earth who have expressed their erroneous opinions down the ages. This is what he said:

"God never meant religion to be a mystery. It is man who has made it so. His handiwork is plain enough for all to understand, and religion was never meant to be in any way different. What should be simple has been made obscure. You have but to do your best—no one can do better, and the future will gradually unfold before you and your duty be made clear."

How much more satisfying is this rational and more natural outlook than that which is taught in the creeds, doctrines and dogmas of Christianity, or any other world religion. Earth religions have produced gods, angels, saints and devils out of those human beings of earth who have passed on, to be considered divine or malign when they have come back to commune with the people of this world. Nevertheless, this book proves them to be human like ourselves, and that many are, like ourselves, still trying to understand more of the mystery of God and of existence.

One who was an unbeliever in any religion when on earth, the fiancé of one of the sitters, once spoke to us in these words:

"I am now trying to do God's Will as far as I can. I do not know exactly what the Will of God is. We never fathom that even on our side, but we reach forward, stage by stage, doing the Father's Will as far as we can grasp it, doing our best to follow the pathway which is directed to us by the Shining Ones above us, knowing that the only road to progress is by doing the will of the Great Ones.

"Have you ever taken into consideration, my friends; of course I cannot go into details about it, but you speak about the Word of God. When you say that, are you speaking about the Bible? If not, I am afraid I have misconstrued your meaning. The Word of God was far before Bible times. You must not have your own understanding of God's Will. I am not speaking about what you believe, it is what you are. (Emphatically said.) May I say this, it is not what the world thinks you are, not what your friends around you think you are, it is what you are within yourself.

"Immediately on passing to this side, and friends have got you really wakened up, you land in a condition suited to your spiritual development, at the stage which you left on the Earth Plane. It is up to your own self and those who are working with you, how you progress thereafter. For every one who passes over there are some dear ones waiting to receive them, but they cannot take them to the condition which they have not reached. They can only meet them at the 'Gateway', and then they have got to say good-bye until those who have just passed reach that condition which they have attained. It is service that is the lever which lifts us all up through the spirit planes."

Another unbeliever in earth religions when he was on earth, returned to tell us that he had found that materialism is not the correct answer to the eternal problem. In answer to a question I put to him after a long conversation he replied:

"I must go now, but before going I would like to tell you, sir, that I was brought up in the Roman Catholic Faith, but I did not come over here as a Roman Catholic. Before coming here I gave up all creeds. I came here a free thinker, but I was wrong in not believing in survival. I came here minus my physical body. When I keep in touch with the earth plane my surroundings are practically on a par with the physical world, but in the higher spheres we get away from earth conditions.

"Now I have for the time being taken on earth conditions, and I am part of your world. I will touch you (I felt a touch on my left arm) and I am conscious of that touch. (Sloan's hands and feet were controlled by me, and the stenographer could not have reached me, in fact, the speaker had no sooner said the words than I felt the touch.) Many of us here in our normal state often touch our friends on earth, and at first are much distressed that no notice is taken of us, forgetting that with our more refined bodies we cannot be seen or felt. I must go now; good-bye!"

An Etherian who had been a Scottish Presbyterian minister in Glasgow returned at times to speak at the Sloan circle. On this occasion, after giving his name to a sitter who had been a member of his church, he said:

"May the peace of the Great Loving Father come nigh to you, to each one of you individually, and give to each one individually the desire of fulfilment of the wish that is closest to the heart, if it be in accordance with Thy Will, O Holy One, and, if it be Thy Will, give them the courage, the strength, and the ability to spread this Truth amongst men, to help them on their journey towards this side of life. Do all in love, if I may put it that way, and commit thy ways unto the Will of the Great Father, and what is for your benefit, and for the benefit of all in earth life, will be granted unto you in accordance with His Will. God bless you all. We are all happy here. Just working, and doing our best to make those we have left behind know that we do not feel the parting so much because we can be in touch with them although they do not always know it."

Such a change from the way he had preached when on earth. The above remarks came from a man who died an orthodox Christian and is now a Unitarian, his trinitarianism, creeds and dogmas, and his earth theology, being passed by as obsolete. Like the others who spoke, he now believed in one God, not in three, thus rejecting the majority opinion of the Council of Nicaea, which produced Christianity as we now know it in 325 A.D., when an assembly of ignorant priests pronounced on the nature of God.

When one of the sitters asked a speaker if he now had any further knowledge of God than he had on earth, the reply he received was this:

"The Kingdom of God, that inner consciousness which emanates from the spirit of the Great Eternal, is within you, and it is in all of you to raise it to an understanding which will help you and help others. God bless you, keep you, and help you to understand. I must go now, but I will come again. I have to go away just from your immediate surroundings, but I shall deem it a favour to come some other time to greet you all again. Your earthly experiences are just a stage in spiritual progress."

Those they call the Masters, or the one they call the Master, are advanced Etherians who come down from their higher to the lower planes to guide and teach. It is a name given on earth to leaders or teachers, but I have never heard the word used by Etherians in a religious sense as it is sometimes used on earth. I mention this because of what a Red Indian once said, and it is interesting to notice how much more emotional the Indians were when speaking on religion than were the more phlegmatic "Europeans" who carried on most of the conversation from the other side.

This is what the Indian said:

"You do not need to go down on your knees to make a strenuous effort to reach the Great Father God. Throw out your thoughts and say: 'Great Father, I need your help. I have come to a part of the road when I can go no further without Thy help. Lead me by the hand,' and the Master will come to the rescue, and someone will be sent to help you. I speak to you all. There are times when difficulties may seem overwhelming. Then say: 'Come, dear Father, into Thy hands I commend my way,' and the spirit friends, Pathfinder and such as he, will come and guide you. I am one of the Indians speaking. It is Greentree."

Pathfinder, another Indian, followed on when Greentree had finished speaking, and said to a gentleman present:

"God bless you, my Brother. May the love of the Great Father be with you and guide you. There were some difficult paths which you had to tread, and there are some little difficulties you will yet have to go through. Put your hand out to the Great Father God, and the guiding Spirit will come and lead you and tell you how to proceed. I am Pathfinder."

It will be noticed throughout this book how they always stress that our character and way of life is what matters, and in the following chapter they tell us the results which follow. Consequently, everyone is wise who follows the advice once given to us, which was in these words:

"You have all but a short time on the Earth Plane, and it is up to you who are there to make the best of your opportunities, walking that pathway in such a way as to bring satisfaction to your own soul and joy to those about you, and, in the everlasting time, rejoicing will be yours when you reach Paradise at last."

When a sitter once asked a friend on the other side

whether certain of his friends, who had passed on, were happy, he received this reply:

"There is no doubt about them being happy. Whether you will be in their condition lies with yourself for your life on earth. I am speaking in a general way. If you do your best, that is all that is expected, and the best can do no better."

How satisfying it is to know that if we do our best, no more can be expected of us. How just and reasonable it is, and yet how different it all is from what has been taught in the past in the name of religion. No one in the past could be sure of his or her destiny, because each was told that at the Second Coming, which might happen any day, one would be taken up to heaven and the other left, some were elected and others were outcasts, some were predestined to glory and others to eternal damnation in flames of fire. All had to remain asleep in the grave until the resurrection and final judgment, when the sheep would be separated from the goats.

Who were the sheep and who were the goats none could be sure, but at least this teaching kept the people fearful and the churches full. Those who were regarded as the faithful, and the most generous, received the most comforting assurances as to their future, while the multitude, unable to think for themselves, accepted what they were told by the priests.

This was profitable for the priesthood who held a high position in the land and, being human, they made the most of the prevailing ignorance. With very limited education the system worked by keeping the masses docile and obedient, and the fear of punishment hereafter doubtless deterred many an evil-doer. Progress, however, was retarded, anything new being attributed to the devil, and many a sorrowing one would have been comforted had knowledge replaced ignorance and the fate of the departed been known as it really was. Unfortunately ignorance still prevails, and, if everyone knew the truth, how much sorrow would be lightened, and how much happier life would be to many who mourn without knowledge.

An Etherian who spoke to a lady sitter at length, and who said he knew her father well in Etheria, concluded a long and interesting talk with these words:

"Just continue, friends, in your walk through life to help others, and all will be well with you. You know, friends, if the world could only realise to-day that it is the Will of God that men should help each other as they go along, the world would go on quite happily without wars, tumult, and disturbances, but it is still far from that."

A lady present once had a long talk with her father in Etheria. What he said on other subjects is given elsewhere, but the following seems suitable for this chapter.

Turning to a gentleman present, he said:

"After all, have you ever thought that life is a noble thing? The possibilities you have in your journey through life to do good, grasp them with both hands, for every one of them is accounted for, my brother, and will assist you when you come to this side."

On another occasion a gentleman present spoke for some minutes with a friend on the other side, and in the course of the conversation this Etherian remarked:

"We aspire for the better, you know, most of us, and if you only let the light, the knowledge of the truth of the Great One, penetrate your soul, and pass that knowledge on to others less fortunate than you are, we shall feel we have accomplished something in the Master's service."

During the Second World War the subject of loving one's enemies was discussed between an Etherian and a lady present. After he had given a long address on this and other subjects, he concluded with these words:

"If you give love to your enemy, well, you are giving love on both sides where it can be used. Had the nations of the world had more love for each other, the world would not be in the state it is in at the present time. God bless you. A thought of love goes to your credit, dear lady, all the time."

A frequent communicator once gave us this advice, which we can also take as comprising his religious beliefs:

"I have been a long time on the spirit side of life, and always try hard to cheer and comfort you before you go away. Never be ashamed to say you know there is a higher life, a God above, a Father, whatever name you may call Him by, who looks after you and guides you, who expects you to do the right thing, to take the right course through life. I did not believe in it myself. You can tell my beloved when you write to her that I have found proof now, and I have come to this little gathering to talk to you and give you a little cheer and comfort."

Each séance usually ended by some kind of farewell and blessing, and this is what we once heard before the voices ceased to speak:

"Bless these Thy beloved people and grant that they may be spared to spread the knowledge of the truth of the continuity of life, and to Thee be all glory now and for ever, Amen, and to our Father God Who has allowed me to participate in the glory and the pleasure of life, in this land of spirit, realising that earth life does not finish all, I give Thee praise, O Eternal One, Amen."

And on another occasion, this is what was said:

"May the Peace of the Great Father God, and the blessed love and fellowship we have with one another, keep you and guard you now and for evermore. Amen. God bless you."

We may gather from the quotations given in this chapter that our friends on the other side become, sooner or later, enlightened Unitarians, believing in one God. They try to follow what is called the Will of God, whatever that may be, but to them, as to many on earth, this is expressed in trying to live a good unselfish righteous life. To them religion and ethics are intertwined, and, from what they tell us, we shall find when we reach the other side that as we sow here we shall reap hereafter.

The basis of orthodox religion is belief. To be saved one must believe something, no matter how little evidence there is for the doctrine. Christians believe that their sins have been washed away by the death of a saviour who suffered for them. "The blood of Jesus Christ his Son cleanseth us from all sin" (1 John, 1-7). This belief is the basis of Christianity, and has been a source of comfort to millions, but it has retarded their ethical development, so much so that the Christian era is classed by historians as the most degraded period in world history.

To rely on a victim who suffered for our sins, and to feel sure of salvation by holding this belief had, and still has, an adverse effect on the ethical outlook of Christendom, so much so that the greatest scoundrels believed they had an equal chance of reaching heaven as had those who lived good and righteous lives. How many millions have been surprised and disappointed when they reached the other world none can say, but the sooner mankind realises that it is what we are that counts in Etheria, and not the theological beliefs we hold, the better it will be for everyone.

CHAPTER XIII

PROGRESS

BY our contact with the etheric world we realise the importance our friends there attach to progress, to mental development, in fact, to the entire evolution of the individual. Moreover, we come to realise that the individual is something infinitely greater than he appears to be on earth.

Opportunities there come to everyone to advance in the ethical way of life, in knowledge, and a better understanding of themselves and the universe in which they live. The handicaps of the grosser vibrations in which we live on earth are removed, the new arrivals learning how to adjust themselves to the finer conditions of their new abode, and live a life of greater intensity, of greater freedom and vitality, such as is unknown to the people of earth.

Freed from the cumbersome physical body, to be able to do much as you think, to find oneself pitched to a higher key and in tune with surroundings of a colour and beauty unrealised on earth, produces a state of harmony and happiness we are unable to appreciate. Always there is a goal ahead of further achievement, but let those who have experienced this wider life tell us about what to us is a wonderland far beyond human imagination.

When I began my enquiries about this other world we all shall some day reach, I was anxious to know if our individuality was preserved. So I asked a friend in Etheria, to whom I was once speaking, if we always retained our individuality, and this was his reply:

"Think of the country-side with glens and hills. The rain falls, and gradually trickles down into small streams, which streams gather volume until they enter a brook, which brook in turn enters a river, which in turn enters a larger river and sweeps onward to the sea. Each individual can be compared to an atom in the raindrop. The atom retains form and individuality throughout the whole course, from the hill to the sea, and even in the sea it does not lose its individuality. So with us, we move onwards and onwards, always retaining our individuality until we merge into the sea of full understanding, when we become part of the Divinity."

On another occasion, someone amongst the sitters mentioned about the improved way an Etherian had just spoken to us, and how much easier it now was to understand what he said. As it turned out, this remark was well chosen, as he came back and made this further interesting statement:

"You know it is the march of evolution, and such a wonderful evolution for me to get away from the cares and troubles of the world, for, when you feast your eyes on the Spirit-land beauties, earth fades into insignificance, except for the loved ones left behind. There is nothing to fear; the only thing I would advise you to do is to prune your earth plumage by good deeds and actions in a quiet unassuming way. You will find that not one of these little actions will be forgotten on this side; gems for your raiment, diamonds for your home. Everyone is reaping the labour of love which he has sown on earth life helping others; it will all go to your heritage in the land of spirit."

Another old friend and frequent communicator said this on another occasion, when speaking on what he called the everlasting progress of the human soul. His preliminary statement is given elsewhere, but this is how he ended his remarks:

"I am perhaps a little further advanced than some of you, but I have still a long, long way to go, and I hope to be able to do something to help you forward on that beautiful journey, on the road that leads upwards and onwards towards the Great and Eternal One."

After a mother in Etheria had spoken to her daughter in the circle, we sat for a few minutes awaiting the next voice to speak to us. Then, out of the silence, a clear manly voice remarked:

"I am just an Indian speaking. I am not like my friend Whitefeather. I have not got the tuition but I have learned, by mixing with the people who come from Higher Spheres, something of those advanced spheres where they live. You know, my friends, in the Spirit World, space is beyond expression. We cannot measure it or limit it, and beyond in space are worlds beyond worlds, all peopled by those who have advanced far beyond us, and we on this side are only on the fringe of that journey towards those spheres where they dwell, gorgeous in their light, their beauty and their love, so that I must fail in my description of them."

On another occasion Whitefeather spoke himself. When Sloan was in trance, Whitefeather was his principal control. However, all the communications recorded in this book, except one, were given by

Etherians who used their own voices by materialising their vocal organs as already explained, and it was in this way that Whitefeather spoke these words, when concluding a talk he had with the lady whose name he mentions :

"I have learned a little and I pay tribute most heartily to your beloved son, Mrs. Lang, who educated me to the language which I now speak, and in the tone in which I now speak, but I am still Whitefeather, the old Whitefeather in heart. Only I have gained a little further knowledge and have progressed a little in the life on our side. God bless you, says Whitefeather."

Here we may have an answer to a problem about which I have often pondered. What has happened to the multitude of beings who have occupied this earth since the time of primitive man? We have discovered something about those who have lived and died within our times, and who were like ourselves, but these are a minute fraction of those who have lived on earth as men, women and children. Going back the fifty thousand years since the time of sub-man, millions and millions of backward primitive people have passed on into the other world, and must occupy some place in what we term space.

If we progress after death, they likewise will have done so, and are still doing so. Life and mental development seem to be closely linked, and if Whitefeather, who on earth was by our standard a simple ignorant Red Indian, can reach the stage he has now attained, why not every one? Why not the primitive black races, the cannibals, the savages, the Australian aborigines, in fact, why should the law of progression favour only the advanced races of mankind?

I remember Whitefeather in 1918. He knew only a few words of English and was simple and childlike, as he doubtless was on earth, yet, as children do, he has grown up to be a man of intelligence and culture, if we judge by what he says.

Education, and the right environment on earth, can work wonders on all mankind, the colour of the skin having nothing to do with the potential power of the mind to develop. This being so, no limit can be placed on the range of the mind and, as an African negro can be educated on earth to become a University Professor, so, by education, the most backward of mankind can develop and progress both here on earth and hereafter in Etheria. As mind can develop here, so it can continue to develop there.

Now we shall proceed and hear more of what they have to say about their progress onwards to a larger, wider life.

After giving a description of the beauties of the plane on which he lives, a friend of one of the sitters said something which shows how death does not all at once change the individual's character or mental development. We are the same individuals just after death as we were before it, it being only the bodily covering which has changed. This is what he said:

"Yes, friends, I am still far from where you are spiritually. I had many stumbles on my way through life, and I fully confessed my faults when I came here to the Great Ones above me, and have been placed in a condition which was much better than I deserved. I am now humbly striving by the little I can do to help, to make up for the faults and failings of earth life, and I get beautiful friends who come to give me advice, to teach me, and lead me on the way to a higher sphere. Meantime I am quite content to do my little best here for the boys who are coming over. I saw the lights, and knew I was in, or near, the Earth Plane, and thought I might bring you a little comfort."

Another who was known to some of those present in the circle once made a similar confession:

"There are few who go through the world straight, and many of the strait-laced ones, when they come to my side of life, will find that they have also left a zig-zag trail behind. I walked a crooked path but I have got behind that now, and somehow there were so many friends on this side of life whom I did not know, but who came to help me when I got here, and have helped me to get to this stage of discernment."

But past mistakes can be corrected. This is what we were once told:

"Freewill, however, obtains even on this side, and it is left to yourself whether you are willing to progress or otherwise. Without that willingness you will not progress very far. I have progressed somewhat myself; but I am a missionary, helping my brothers and sisters over the stile all I can."

When an Etherian was once asked what his work was, he replied in the pure Scotch dialect which, translated into English, reads thus:

"When I am not required for the Great Elder Brother's work, I come to this earth side, and try to help those of my own kind, not exactly friends, although they are all friends of mine, but if I can give anyone a helping hand over a stile, I am rewarded myself a thousand times."

"That is how you progress," said someone in the circle in reply, to which he answered in these words:

"It is the only way, but I do not want to progress very far for a bit. It is my desire to stay here because I have some friends I want to wait for. Oh, I loved them well. It is given unto us, if we do what we are told, and behave ourselves, and all work for the Master and the Elder Brothers, to stay a little while where we are until they come. God help me, I loved them awful well. Sometimes, friends, those that are left without a father's care canna keep straight, and I am trying to bring them back on to the right road again, those who have gone off the straight a little way. You can overdo the things of earth life, you know, at times. I think you understand what I mean, and it is so very, very easy to step aside."

A Red Indian, already known to us by the name of "Pathfinder", came often to the circle and could speak with ease for a quarter of an hour or more. After giving a long address he was asked once if his interests lay solely on the earth plane, to which he replied:

"No, I work on both sides—on the Earth Plane and also on the lower planes on this side. I have progressed to a higher plane myself, but am doing this work for the Master's sake. The fields are ripe for the harvest, but sometimes the reapers are few. In God's Garden of Life, however, there are many helpers and workers in the fields of Paradise who go out to help their weaker brothers and sisters. It is one of the Indian friends speaking. I am Pathfinder. I have found a path that led me to higher heights, more beautiful and glorious heights, my lovely home, but I thought of those left behind and prayed that I might be allowed for a little time to act as pathfinder for my brothers and sisters who need help when they come to this side of life."

On one occasion the members of the circle were discussing amongst themselves, during a silence on the other side, the ignorance and antipathy of the clergy, and of Christians in general, to the truths proclaimed by Spiritualism. A gentleman present remarked that their outlook would retard their progress when they reached the other side, until they discarded their false beliefs. Then it was that an Etherian joined in the conversation and spoke these words:

"That is very true, Mr. Cameron. It is not only our own progress on the spirit side of life that we must think of, but we come in contact with many that have not come so far as we have, and we try to help them. Then, in turn, we come into contact with those a long way ahead of us on the road of life, and the knowledge we gain we owe to them."

After a friend in Etheria had told us once how he had endeavoured to make up for his failings during his life on earth, one of us remarked that only by so doing could progress be made. To this he replied:

"It is the only way of progression. By helping others we help ourselves. There are many, many friends who are much superior to me in their spiritual outlook that I have not overtaken yet. I have seen them, and talked to them as you are talking to me now, and I am doing the best I can to make myself fit, to attune myself to their sphere. When I do so I shall be with them, and it will be a joyous day when it does come."

The subject of progress came up on another

occasion when we were told about passing from one plane to another. What was said is given elsewhere, but here is the place to quote the words of an Etherian about his own personal feelings against leaving his present abode:

"What I will ultimately attain to I do not know, but I am quite content to remain where I am at present, and to progress slowly from time to time and feel the vision which is opening up to me so wonderfully. When we traverse the spaces with these brighter ones and communicate with those who have gone on, we get glimpses of the glories to come. I would not, however, be content there. I want to get back to my own associates and to the places where I am established at the present time, and wait for the loved ones who are still on your side of life."

A man who was a famous scientist on earth, and who did much to popularise the belief in the evolution of the species, came back several times to speak to me. He always gave his name, and what he once said is suitable for inclusion in this chapter. This is how he concluded his talk:

"Evolution is still my great theme, the thing I am constantly thinking about. Evolution is the key to the Universe. Evolution never ends. We are always progressing, progressing, but we retain our individuality. It helps to explain the mystery of existence."

He has now realised the mistake he made when on earth of denouncing Spiritualism, and here I take the opportunity, now that this book is drawing to a close, of asking this question. Can any sensible person assert that all the 419 quotations given on its pages were spoken by someone living on earth, in the room where the séances were held? If neither the medium, nor one or more of the people present, produced the voices, who did? Whence did all we have read come? The circle was a small one, some eight or nine people on an average, and no one could speak without it being noticed, and yet for over forty years no one ever hinted that the medium, or anybody else, was pretending to speak as somebody other than himself or herself.

There could be no gadget, contrivance or device to produce the voices from elsewhere by an accomplice. No one, for instance, could produce the voices through a hole in the wall, make them to sound in front of the sitter, and hear what the sitter said and carry on a conversation. When the séance was held in Sloan's own sitting-room it was always searched and any such contrivance would soon have been spotted, but it must be remembered that many of his séances were held in the private houses of people where such devices could not have been installed. Moreover, a number of good evidential séances were held under my direction in the séance-room of the Glasgow Society for Psychical Research, and when Sloan arrived he entered the room immediately, sat down, and was never alone until he left at the end of the séance.

Sloan's conversation was slow and halting, and it showed no special knowledge of anything beyond his everyday interests, and yet hundreds of thousands of fluent words have been heard, to make up the wonderful and extraordinary communications the people present listened to all these years. As to the possibility of someone in the circle impersonating different dead people, that was impossible, as the voices spoke no matter who was present. Those who made up the circle were always changing, and over forty years the entire make-up of the circle changed very many times.

The extracts given in this book cover séances held over twenty-seven years, the first recorded being on 20th September, 1918, and the last on 10th July, 1945. Nevertheless the same phenomena took place at the first as at the last. Those Etherians who spoke in 1918 had the same personalities as they had in 1945, the same facts were given about their world and how they lived, and the same elevated teaching continued all those years. The trumpet continued to race about the room in the same way and touch, but never hurt, anyone. Spotlights continued to move about the room, the consistency of everything is noteworthy, and yet the members of the circle had changed over and over again, many having passed on to become in turn the speakers from the other side.

In the later years of his life Sloan's memory was failing and he had aged, to become a lonely old man whose uppermost thoughts were the prospect of soon being taken to the other world, to be once more with his beloved wife. He suffered from rheumatism and the disabilities of old age, and yet the final sittings he gave, when he was seventy-six years of age, were amongst the best ever held. Nevertheless this remarkable man always refused payment and shunned publicity to the last, passing away peacefully on 24th May, 1951, at eighty-two years of age, quite unaware of how much his life had meant to humanity.

Now to return to the subject of this chapter. Once

in the course of a conversation with a friend on the other side, one of the sitters used the word "evolution", which was just the word the Etherian wanted. He was so pleased, and this is what he said:

"Precisely, evolution; that is the correct word. They are not all at the same stage of advancement. It is just what happens all the time. We are just evolving from one stage of spiritual existence to another and become more perfect, and so more able to help others below us. At the present time I am working amongst those who are passing through war. I am often mixing with them, and telling them, directing them where they should go. The plane in which I live is a little more beautiful than theirs. I mean I should be on a more exalted plane, but I have chosen to do that work and be with them meantime."

Another aspect of progress was once put to us by an Etherian in these words:

"It comes overwhelmingly upon us when we see intelligences so far ahead of us, and we desire to follow in the footsteps of the Great Master Teacher. In method of progress it means assimilation of the Truth which we must take unto ourselves, and that we are willing to obey the will of those above us, and follow in the higher footsteps of those advanced far beyond us. It is not a theme of a day, as you call it, a month or a year. It is of long duration before some rise to this discernment. Do you see what I mean? The urge to rise has no limitation. It remains with us, our desire to follow in the steps of the great teachers who have gone ahead."

I once asked a friend who was speaking to me

from Etheria if everyone there could make contact with this earth. To this enquiry he replied:

"The higher and more developed we become the less are we in touch with your world. The more development proceeds the less do we think of the earth. It is all a question of desire. We can come into contact with earth conditions at will; if the will for doing so is absent then we do not return to you."

In other words the memory of our earth life gradually fades until our earth life is forgotten, and this seems to me to be an answer to those who believe in reincarnation. Once I put the straight question, "Do we reincarnate again on earth?"—to which I received this reply from the Etherian to whom I was speaking:

"I have known no one who has been re-incarnated on earth. I passed over many years ago, and I have round about me those who lived thousands of years ago on earth. That is all I can say, because my knowledge does not permit me to say more."

Another equally unequivocal reply on the same subject was given by a different Etherian some years later. He said:

"We cannot come back and go through the same again."

What they talk about is progress, and never have I heard anyone on the other side speak of coming back to be born again on earth. The butterfly cannot return to enter the cocoon. Remarks like the following were quite common:

"I was an Indian Chief in the old days. I have now been on the spirit side of life for many years as you know time."

A lady present on one occasion was greeted by the man to whom she had been engaged on earth before his passing over. Like the others who spoke to us, when referring to being reunited some day with those they love on earth, the same remark was made, namely, that when they meet again there will be no more parting. This is what he said:

"You know what dark days are, Mary, and I know what dark days are too, but there is a glorious day to follow, which has already dawned on me, and which must dawn some time on you also. Daybreak will shine; brightness will come; be of good cheer, darling, I will stand by you.

"When the long last comes, which I hope may not be for a long time yet and that much happiness may still be your lot in the earth life, but when the time does come, dearest, then at the end of the road we shall clasp hands again. There will be no more partings, no more worry, no more care. Hand in hand, through the aeons of eternity, with spiritual love in our hearts, we will help others along and find service and joy in that work. God bless you, darling; no more just now."

The same theme ran through the remarks made to a sitter by her mother in Etheria. It was the sitter's birthday, and her mother's good wishes were given in these words, to end with the daughter feeling that she had been kissed many times:

"It is a memorable day, Crissie. It was a memorable day to me and to Father too. I was just waiting a chance, my darling, to get in to wish you "many happy returns of the day" until that birthday comes when you will come over to our side of life, and you and I will be together for all eternity. I just want you to understand."

Then addressing the others present in the circle she said:

"What happy times Crissie and I will have when she leaves the physical. I was not able to enter into all the enjoyments that she could enter into before I went away. I was a wee bit forgetful sometimes, but before that we were just like sisters, not like mother and daughter."

After a Red Indian had finished talking, a gentleman present once asked someone on the other side if it was possible to take the less developed to the higher planes. This is what he was told by the Etherian, who spoke in a loud clear voice:

"We cannot take them, but we tell them what is in store for them, and that when they become more enlightened they can go there. It is not the Indian who is speaking now, but I am not speaking disparagingly in any way. Many Indians are more advanced and have brighter souls than I have. We are all brothers and sisters, and we all have a time of what one might call evening star—that time of the last final parting with the Earth Plane, and we say good-bye to all things earthly, so to speak. One goes a little adrift for a little while until one finds one's bearings, or, I should say until some of the beautiful shining ones meet you and point the way, and tell you where you should go. You have all got to work out your own destiny. There is no doubt about it, work out your own Heaven, and rest assured the Great Father will see your labour, and reward you for it."

Then the speaker paused for a moment and continued:

"That is what happens as you will find when you come to my side of life. You have still to seek further knowledge. It would not be a real world on this side unless there was progress and still further progress, and those who have gone a little ahead, in advance, can always help the stragglers upwards as they go along. They are not all fit to start at a high level, they need a helping hand, and these helping hands are never far away.

"One meets all classes and conditions of friends on this side of life, and each and all require a helping hand. You cannot transform a soul immediately from the lower grade which he has left to a celestial grade. It is a gradual spiritual progress, and they are always obtaining fresh knowledge and fresh hope from those who are a little further advanced than they are, and who are always very willing to help a weaker brother up towards the brighter and more shining light."

He had still much more to say but this is given elsewhere, in fact his talk was more in the nature of an address, as it lasted for ten minutes.

Once the question was put about the different stages of development the people were in on the other side. Someone asked an Etherian, who was a healer of earth people by means of healing rays, if undeveloped bodies are ever to be seen in Etheria, and this was the reply:

"Not undeveloped. The stage of development is seen by the light or the brightness, the shades of light. We see them in different stages of advancement, and talk with them. There are many beautiful passengers who talk with us at times, and we get great enlightenment from them."

He then went on to tell how the etheric body has the same formation as the physical body, and that everyone has a perfect etheric body. His remarks will be found elsewhere. Then he returned to the subject of mental development and concluded with these words:

"Those who have not developed much in earth life just have to rise gradually, and those who have not had any spiritual development are generally taken to spheres where they can be ministered to in the way that they most need."

Towards the close of a long address on various subjects an Etherian spoke these words:

"If you have a will to travel in the spheres in God's service in the spirit side of life, you will find ample opportunity, if you are willing to work for the Master, but you will have to comply with his laws and the conditions of life which exist on the spirit side. You cannot take a hop, step, and jump, from the side of life which you are on just now, right to the celestial spheres on the spirit side of life. It is Work, Service and Love, which will bring joy and harmony and peace into your inmost souls. Of course, you will always have the knowledge that you are helping someone whom you know has not just reached the stage you have reached, and you will reach out a helping hand to help them up, and those on the higher plane above will immediately put out their hands to help you on a further step again.

"Progress all the time, until, in God's good time,

you reach the fulfilment of a purified soul, that can work in harmony with the Great Spirit of All Life. Progress will go on until the full theme and completion of the Master's Will is accomplished, and you are able to mix with those Shining Ones, in a glorified condition, whom you hope to join some day.

"There is a stage when some of us can know no further. There is a world inside another world, but we have not progressed to that knowledge, nor will we, until we have advanced to a stage much above our present knowledge."

When a sitter once said that he liked to be able to give reasons for his belief in Spiritualism, he was told by a friend on the other side:

"Never argue. Don't, if you take my advice, my Brother. Rather tell them about the beauties of this life which you will discover. You are really just an explorer seeking out a new country, and you have acquired a mind which can see and glean something of the beauty of this land, which many others cannot. You will link up with those who have advanced beyond you by and by, and will learn from them.

"As the Great Master said: 'In my Father's house are many mansions,' and you are only going to the place which you in earth life, by your life on earth, have prepared yourself for, and then you will progress afterwards by getting into touch with those advanced ones who are ready to help you, and to give you knowledge of things which you do not know, but which will be given to you as you can assimilate and understand them. I am just putting it in the best way I can, and I hope you follow what I mean."

During the Second World War the thoughts of most people were directed to the host of young men, all over the world, who were being ushered into a new life before they had had time to grasp the meaning of this life on earth. What kind of life awaited this multitude of new arrivals, was once asked by one of us, and this is what we were told:

"It depends much upon the condition of their life before they came to this side, and their inclination to aspire to the higher life. If they have not had that desire in earth life, they will not so speedily advance."

Our future, both in this life and in the next, depends on ourselves alone. As we are here, so shall we be there. Our sowing, if good, produces a bountiful harvest, but, if bad, the reverse. If we are selfish on earth we shall be selfish there. Selfishness is the root of all evil, just as unselfishness is the root of all that is good. Our happiness, or unhappiness, springs from our attitude towards ourselves and to others. No one can save us from our own wickedness and folly, and what we are, and what we become, is for each one to decide for himself or herself.

The ancient Egyptians placed in the coffins of the deceased a guide to the next world, wherein was depicted the path the newly arrived soul was to take before he reached the abode of the god Osiris, the judge of the dead. There he was weighed in the balance, and all the good and evil he had done was revealed. The good passed into heaven and the evil into hell. Doubtless this belief encouraged many to live more righteous lives, as it is known that its effect on individual conduct was good, but the guide so dwells on the dangers and difficulties the newly arrived soul has to encounter, the many devils who waylay him, that one wonders how he ever reached his goal.

When theology is called in to explain the mystery of death and the hereafter, we may be sure that what is simple will be made difficult, and what is clear will be made obscure. The only way to arrive at the truth is to hear, or read for ourselves, what those who have gone before have to tell us. Thus we find that the smokescreen of doubt, difficulty and uncertainty put up by all the different world religions is due to ignorance, and, when we keep to what our friends in Etheria have to tell us, the road ahead of us is clear and simple for all to understand.

As we have already read, our duty in life is to do our best, the highest wisdom is to do good, and, if we do that to the utmost of our ability, our future is bright. Then the universe will slowly unfold before us, and our journey through the spheres, from plane to plane in the ages to come, will bring happiness to ourselves and all with whom we come in contact. There seems to be no end to the way of life.

No one could have put in fewer or better words what Spiritualism stands for than did Joseph Addison, a contemporary of Swedenborg, a great man of letters, a man of real goodness as well as of eminent genius, who wrote:

> "To look upon the soul as going on from strength to strength, to consider that it is to shine forever with new accessions of glory, and brighten to all eternity; that it will be still adding virtue to virtue, and knowledge to knowledge, carries in it something wonderfully agreeable to that ambition which is natural to the mind of man."